# SPRING WORLD,
## AWAKE

# SPRING WORLD, AWAKE

*Stories, Poems, and Essays Compiled by*
MILDRED CORELL LUCKHARDT
ILLUSTRATED BY RALPH McDONALD

655

ABINGDON PRESS
Nashville and New York

THE COMPILER AND PUBLISHERS WISH TO THANK INDIVIDUALS AND PUBLISHERS
FOR THEIR PERMISSION TO USE COPYRIGHTED MATERIAL AS FOLLOWS:

Abingdon Press for "The Shout in the Valley" from *The Teakwood Pulpit and Other Stories* by Alice Geer Kelsey. Story copyright © 1949 assigned to Abingdon Press.

Angus & Robertson Ltd. for "The Bush" by A. B. Paterson and "Earth's Youngest Daughter" by M. Finnin.

Associated Book Publishers Ltd. and the Bodleian Library, Oxford, for "The River Bank" from *The Wind in the Willows* by Kenneth Grahame, published by Methuen and Company, Ltd., London, and Charles Scribner's Sons, New York.

Lorraine Babbitt, for the poems "Tree Portraits" and "Cactus Kingdom."

Behrman House, Inc. for "Joyful Springtime Holidays—Passover and Shavuoth"

from *The Story of the Synagogue* by Meyer Levin and Toby K. Kurzband.

Bloch Publishing Company for "Habibi and Yow Go to Grandfather's House for Seder," from *Habibi and Yow* by Althea O. Silverman, and "Spring Festivals—Shabuoth and Passover" from *With the Jewish Child in Home and Synagogue* by Elma Ehrlich Levinger.

The Bobbs-Merrill Company, Inc. for "April Comes to the Coast of Maine" and "May Comes to a Salt Water Farm on the Maine Coast" from *Coast Calendar* by Robert P. Tristram Coffin, copyright, 1947, 1949 by The Bobbs-Merrill Company, Inc.; and for "When Early March Seems Middle May" from *The Biographical*

Alice Geer Kelsey for "Candles at Midnight."

Alfred A. Knopf, Inc. for "In Time of Silver Rain," copyright 1938 and renewed 1966 by Langston Hughes, reprinted from *Fields of Wonder* by Langston Hughes; "April Rain Song" from *The Dream Keeper* by Langston Hughes, copyright 1932 by Alfred A. Knopf, Inc. and renewed 1960 by Langston Hughes; "A Dime's Worth for Free," copyright 1949 by Marion Holland, reprinted from *Billy Had a System* by Marion Holland; and "The Hare and the Hedgehog" from *Tales Told Again* by Walter de la Mare, copyright 1927 and renewed 1955 by Walter de la Mare.

J. B. Lippincott Company for "The First Lamb" from *Children of North America* by Louise A. Stinetorf. Copyright, 1943, by Louise A. Stinetorf.

Lutterworth Press, British Publishers of *By the Shores of Silver Lake* by Laura Ingalls Wilder.

The Macmillan Company for "The White Blackbird" from *The Peep Show Man* by Padraic Colum, copyright 1924 by The Macmillan Company, renewed 1952 by Padraic Colum; "How the Little Owl's Name Was Changed" from *Beyond the Clapping Mountains* by Charles E. Gillham, copyright 1943 by The Macmillan Company.

McClelland and Stewart, Ltd., for "Daisies" by Bliss Carman from *Bliss Carman's Poems.*

McGraw-Hill Book Company and Jesse Stuart for "April Night and the Singing Winds," "Hold April," "Ides of March," and "Spring World, Awake," from *Hold April,* copyright © 1962 by Jesse Stuart; and for "Spring Comes to the Kentucky Hills," excerpts from *The Year of My Rebirth,* copyright © 1956 by Jesse Stuart. Used by permission of the author and the publishers.

Meredith Press for "The Flower-Fed Buffaloes" from *Going to the Stars* by Vachel Lindsay, copyright, 1926 by D. Appleton & Company, renewed 1954 by Elizabeth C. Lindsay; by permission of Appleton-Century, affiliate of Meredith Press.

New Directions Publishing Corporation for "Priapos of the Harbor" by Antipater of Sidon from *Poems from the Greek Anthology* by Dudley Fitts, copyright 1938, 1941, 1956 by New Directions.

W. W. Norton & Company, Inc. for "New England May Day" from *The White Gate* by Mary Ellen Chase, copyright 1954 by Mary Ellen Chase.

Oxford University Press for "Daffodils" from *A Year of Japanese Epigrams* by W. N. Porter.

Laurence Pollinger Ltd. for "A Prayer in Spring" by Robert Frost from *The Complete Poems of Robert Frost,* published in the British Commonwealth by Jonathan Cape Ltd.

Smithsonian Institution Press for "Song of the Chippewa Medicine Man" from *Making Maple Sugar,* collected by Frances Densmore, Bureau of American Ethnology, Smithsonian Institution.

The Society of Authors for "The Hare and the Hedgehog" by Walter de la Mare, reprinted by permission of the Literary Trustees of Walter de la Mare and The Society of Authors as their representative; and for "Loveliest of Trees" by A. E. Housman, reprinted by permission of The Society of Authors as the literary representative of the Estate of A. E. Housman and of Jonathan Cape Ltd., publishers of A. E. Housman's *Collected Poems.*

Viking Press, Inc., for "Ground Hog Sees His Shadow" from *Miss Hickory* by Carolyn Sherwin Bailey, copyright 1946 by Carolyn Sherwin Bailey.

Western Publishing Company, Inc. for "Yo Han and the Baby Camel" by Adelaide Truesdell, copyright 1946 by *Story Parade, Inc.*

The World Publishing Company for "When Wandering Time Is Come" from *Beyond the High Hills* by Knud Rasmussen, copyright © 1961 by The World Publishing Company.

TO

*Doris Bird, Children's Librarian,*
*Rye Library, Rye, New York,*
*friend of countless girls and boys*

*and to*
*Allison, Amy, Betsy, Bill, Bruce, Corell,*
*Douglas, Francie, Gordon, Lucy Anne,*
*Marianne, Nan, and Richard*

*and to*
*the many girls and boys in a number of places*
*who have welcomed me to their*
*schools and libraries and talked with me about books*

*May each one of you*
*together with people in every land*
*enjoy the wonders of springtime*
*and of every season throughout the year.*

## Thank You, One and All,

who, from many places throughout the world, have responded so generously to my plea for help in preparing this book and have sent me springtime material and given me all kinds of assistance and encouragement. In gathering these selections I have made new friends from far away and near at home and strengthened old friendships, for all of which I am grateful.

Since it would be impossible to list the names of all the girls and boys, their parents, teachers, and librarians, together with many other persons who have aided me I shall list only a few here; and those who are not mentioned must remember that I am thankful for the various ways in which they have helped me in my writing.

Special thanks are due to those whose names follow: Miss Suzanne Mourot, Deputy Mitchell Librarian, Mitchell Library, and Mrs. Noreen Shelley, editor of "School Magazine," Sydney, Australia; Miss Janet A. Hill, Borough Children's Librarian, London Borough of Lambeth, London, England; Padre John M. Donahue,

M.M., Puno, Peru, S.A.; Miss Vrinda Telang, Bombay, India; Miss Rarinthorn Bhantsbha, Bangkok, Thailand; Miss Doris Scott, Librarian, Boys and Girls House, Toronto Public Libraries, Toronto, Canada; Frank Kujawinski, Anayama, Ivory Coast, Africa;

From Huntsville, Alabama, Mrs. Thomas Darling and Mrs. Dorothy Hendry, faculty adviser for the High School "Spectrum," Miss Holly Geer and Mr. George Rebh, students; Mrs. Martin Hibbs and Mr. Don Pinney, Literature and History Division, and Mr. Clyde Brown of the Saguaro Branch, all of Phoenix, Arizona Public Library System; Mrs. Philip Luckhardt and her daughters, Scottsdale, Arizona; Miss Charlotte Harriss, assistant reference librarian, California State Library, Sacramento; from Easton, Connecticut, Miss Evelyn Krakow's fourth grade class in Staples School, and Miss Betsy Kenney, Miss Marianne Kenney, and Mrs. David Kenney, teacher, all of Helen Keller Middle School; Mrs. Anthony Wayne Mazzarella, teacher, Orlando, Florida;

Miss Susan Taylor, State Consultant, Children's Services, Department of Education, Honolulu, Hawaii; Mrs. Kenneth Larrabee, Librarian, Merrill Memorial Library, Yarmouth, Maine, and Mrs. Catherine Cates, Circulation Librarian, Maine State Library, Augusta, Maine; girls and boys in Liljas School, Natick, Massachusetts; Mrs. Alfred Low, teacher, Peoria, Illinois; Mrs. Frances Lux, Kansas City, Missouri; Dr. Arna Bontemps, Nashville, Tennessee;

Girls and boys in Marlborough Elementary School, Marlborough, New Hampshire, and their teachers, Mrs. Marie Forcier, Mrs. Esther LaChance, and Mrs. Dorothy Ledwith; Dr. and Mrs. Lawrence K. Hall of Center Sandwich, New Hampshire; Miss Allison Barclay, Riverton, New Jersey; Miss Dorothy Fritz, educational consultant and author, Santa Fe, New Mexico;

Students in Alexander Burger J. H. S. 139 in the City of New

York, and their English teacher, Mrs. Vivian Appel, and their Librarian, Mrs. Eloise Shelton; also the Burger seventh grade student, Rosalyn Harrison, who told to me the story "May Day for Neighbors" in this book; Rabbi Sidney L. Regner, executive vice president, Central Conference of American Rabbis, New York.

Miss Anne Izard, Children's Services Consultant, Westchester Library System, and several other librarians in Westchester County, New York, including Miss Marion Farquharson, Librarian in New Rochele Public Library; librarians in Rye Public Library, especially Miss Doris Bird and Miss Mary Lyon; also from Rye, New York, the Rev. Dr. and Mrs. Deane Edwards; Miss Letitia Jordan; Mr. Paul Smart; Mrs. Morton Snyder; and Rabbi Robert A. Rothman, D.H.L., Community Synagogue, Rye;

Mrs. Myles Chelimer, educator, of Larchmont, New York; Sister Anne Therese Flood, Convent of St. Anne, York, Pennsylvania; Mr. Richard McDowell, faculty member of St. Michael's College, Winooski, Vermont; and Mrs. William Herbert Kibler of Morganton, North Carolina.

To Jesse Stuart, poet, author, educator, and lecturer go very special thanks for his generosity and encouragement while this book was being compiled; and to my husband, "Thank you, again" for helping in many ways, including beating a path to the post office with my hundreds of letters connected with collecting material and searching for reprint permissions.

I hope all these people who have helped me with my writing and everyone who reads this book will share in the joy of springtime whenever it awakens the part of our world in which you live. Also, may you and all whom you meet watch for and enjoy the wonders of each season of the year wherever you are.

—MILDRED CORELL LUCKHARDT

# CONTENTS

# In the Spring

Spring begins officially in the northern half of the world about March 21, when the sun's center crosses the equator from the south to the north. This is known as the vernal or spring equinox, when night and day are equal in length. In the southern hemisphere, spring begins about September 23, but whatever the date people welcome springtime in special ways.

In the United States of America people begin to talk about and to dream about spring long before March 21. Even on February 2, says a familiar folktale, the humble groundhog peeps out of his warm burrow, deep in the earth, to see if spring is coming. If the sun is shining and the groundhog sees his shadow, he returns to his burrow to await the "six more weeks of bad weather." But, oh, if the day is overcast and no shadows trouble the groundhog, spring is on its way!

Spring means many things to many people, but the word itself implies rapid or sudden emerging. The soil is growing warmer, buds appear on trees and bushes, and the first tender shoots of grass press upward. The animals which have been hibernating awaken and stretch to think pleasantly, no doubt, of the good days ahead; many animals are born in the spring. The natural migration of animals and birds and fish begins. There are swift thaws, resulting sometimes in flooded rivers and streams. In some areas spring brings maple-sugaring, seed-planting, and, tree-planting days, and everywhere it brings a sense of renewal, of new life and new dreams. Birds which have spent the winter in warmer climes return and busily begin to build nests—long-legged storks are eagerly awaited in certain European countries where they sometimes build their nests on houses and are said to bring good luck. The return of the swallows to San Juan Capistrano, California, is often greeted by hundreds of watchers. Arctic terns, the birds which migrate from one polar region to another, live in the sunshine longer than any other birds.

Fish leave the ocean to swim up inland streams to spawn. Salman "runs" bring springtime excitement to the Pacific coast. Along the Atlantic coast in the southern part of the United States shad start swimming upstream early in the spring. As spring moves northward, the shad move into the northern streams, and where shad are "running," there may be found also the feathery white shadbush or the shadblow blossoms.

Every state in the United States has its own festivals to welcome spring blossoms. Many such festivals are celebrated in other countries, too. Only a few can be mentioned here, and each reader of this book will think of many more in his own locality and elsewhere.

In the South spring brings a special beauty with the azalea and dogwood. There the peak blooming time for azaleas extends from February, in Texas and along the Gulf coast, to May and June in the Virginia and North Carolina mountains.

A fabled azalea trail attracts countless visitors to Natchez, Mississippi, and nearby towns. Azalea festivals are held in many other places, one being in Wilmington, North Carolina, the first week in April. Charleston, South Carolina, famous for the oldest landscaped gardens in America, is host to thousands of spring visitors who come to enjoy the beauty of azalea, magnolia, and dogwood.

Dogwood is the state flower of North Carolina. In late April and early May shortly after pink azaleas bloom along the Blue Ridge Parkway and on the mountains, dogwood brings added beauty to this scenic state. Many towns and villages in North Carolina hold blossom festivals for azaleas, laurel, rhododendron, and dogwood.

In mid-April in Atlanta, Georgia, almost every street, residence, park, church, and school is beautiful with delicate pink or white dogwood blossoms. People watch the dogwood parade, listen to the spring concerts, wander along dogwood paths, and participate in many special events which are a part of the Atlanta Dogwood Festival.

Cities and towns in other states also pay tribute to the arrival of flowers. A famous dogwood festival takes place on Greenfield Hill in Fairfield, Connecticut, several weeks after the Southern celebrations. Every year many people await the announcement of the date when the dogwood will bloom on Greenfield Hill, and then for a whole week visitors drive slowly along the winding roads, taking pictures of the dogwood-lined stone walls surrounding spacious white New England houses and widespread lawns. Later they gather on the lawn of the picturesque white church for lunch or supper in a fairyland of blossoms.

The arrival of apple blossoms, and the blossoms of the cherry, orange, peach, and plum trees, and various other trees, are joyful occasions in many parts of the United States as in other countries. When the cherry trees, which were a gift to the United States from Japan, bloom in Washington, D.C., the accompanying festival serves to remind countless visitors of the ways in which countries have shared their flowers and trees. When towns in New Hampshire and other New England states are holding lilac festivals, the story is told about the first lilacs which were brought to America from Asia by captains of sailing ships who wanted their families to enjoy the beauty and fragrance of these lovely blossoms. The tulip festivals, such as the famous one in Holland, Michigan, also remind everyone of the journeys that blossoms have made to enhance other countries. The ancestral bulbs of tulips were grown centuries ago in Turkey. Much later, tulips were carried to Europe, where they were greatly treasured, and finally some came to the "New World."

Apple blossom festivals recall John Chapman, who was to become known as "Johnny Appleseed." Born in Massachusetts about 1775, he later followed the covered-wagon trail and traveled throughout the region of the Ohio Valley and as far west as Iowa, giving away seeds for fruit trees and helping plant apple orchards. He is honored every spring at many Arbor Day or tree-planting ceremonies. Apple blossom time is an occasion for crowning a lovely queen in Winchester, Virginia, and there are blossom trails bordering apple orchards in many states.

Rose festivals are held in some parts of the United States—in Tyler, Texas, and Thomasville, Georgia, in early spring—with Newark, New York, celebrating some weeks later and Portland, Oregon, in early June.

The beauty of the springtime in the West has been the inspiration of many poems and stories and one popular song, "When It's Springtime in the Rockies" by Maryhale Woolsey, has been enjoyed by lonesome cowboys on the range and by great crowds in busy cities.

Spring is the wonderful occasion, too, for people to pledge anew their faith in God and mankind. The greatly inspiring festivals of Easter and Passover bring joy and hope and many happy customs.

Springtime religious festivals have been held throughout the world since ancient times. Ramadan is the great Moslem festival observed by countless Moslems in many countries. This period of penance, prayer, and fasting lasts about a month during which Moslems fast all day but may eat at night. At the end of Ramadan there is a three-day festival when gifts are given and received and colorful parades are held.

Although the ancient origins of water festivals may have been forgotten, water rituals still are a part of spring and harvest in many countries. Many people once believed that by sprinkling water they could bring rain for the crops. Fire also is a part of spring festivals in some places. In ancient times the lighting of fires was thought to drive away cold weather and bring back the sunshine with its warmth.

Seed planting and the blessing of young animals have long been connected with spring festivals in various world religions. Often the festivals include delightful parades of animals. The old Rogation Day ritual is being revived by some Christians. The word "rogation" means petition or request, and the ceremony of rogation (asking God's blessing on the fruits of the earth) was introduced by Saint Mamertus, when he was Bishop of Vienne in Gaul, about A.D. 473. Later the custom spread across the English Channel and to other lands. In one Rogation Sunday celebration, held in Pennsylvania in May, farmers along the Conestoga Valley join girls, boys, men, and women in the ceremonies which begin at Bangor Episcopal Church in Churchtown. Those taking part in the ceremony bring bags of seed, calves, lambs, kids, and other young animals for the "blessing of the seeds" and the "blessing of the animals."

Celebrations of freedom, or the struggle for freedom, are very much a part of springtime. Passover, already mentioned as a religious festival, is the oldest and most famous of the freedom festivals. Beginning in Africa more than three thousand years ago, it was carried by the Hebrews to Asia, and is known all over the world.

April 19, 1775, was a landmark in freedom. As Patriot's Day, it is a spring holiday in Massachusetts and some other New England states. For a part of the celebration, Paul Revere's historic ride is recalled vividly by means of a twenty-six mile marathon from Hopkinton to Boston. People of all ages, including many college athletes, start off at noon in a great crowd as the race begins. Along the way spectators cheer them on and bring them water and cold drinks. College girls, boy scouts, girl scouts, civic organizations, school children on holiday, businessmen, and homemakers all are out to watch and cheer on Patriot's Day.

In Switzerland, on the Friday after Ascension, usually some time in May, people make pilgrimages to the shrine of their national hero William Tell, whose courage stirred the forest cantons to strive for independence.

In past springtimes in Switzerland, when the open-air legislative assembly of Canton Uri met, the voters marched out to the meadow in procession. At the head were two men dressed in medieval costumes. Known as the two Tells, in memory of the archer and his son, each carried on his shoulder the horn of a bull—the same horns, it was claimed, which ancient warriors of Uri bore with them in battle. Next came a detachment of soldiers with banners and music, followed by officials and voters. The ceremony still is observed though in less dramatic fashion. And when spring comes to New Glaris, Wisconsin there are extensive rehearsals for the splendid

William Tell play, which is a wellknown summer attraction. At Interlaken in Michigan springtime is a season for rehearsals, sometimes including *"William Tell,"* a summertime offering at this famous music festival.

Spring brings memorable days all over the world. In the United States May 13 marks the anniversary of the settling of Jamestown, Virginia. And on the thirtieth day of May we pay tribute to the men who gave their lives for our country.

Throughout the world spring is a time concerned with freedom.

Springtime brings outdoor sports and games—kites, marbles, jump ropes, hopscotch, hoops, tennis, and baseball practice. Spring is the time of circuses, fairs, and April Fool's Day; May Day, May queens, Maypoles, and daisy chains. And when all the earth is awakening with new life and new energy, it is a perfect time for new dreams and new hopes.

The stories and poems which follow represent the thoughts and talents of many people, some of them well known, some not so well known, but all of them touched by the wonder, by the joyousness which comes in the spring.

—MILDRED CORELL LUCKHARDT

*Rejoice in the annual happening;*
*For all of the world comes another spring.*
—ANNE MARX

# Spring World, Awake

Too late, Spring World, to sleep beneath a cover!
  Wake now beneath your blanket of thin frost!
Pairs of nest-searching crows are flying over
  And not for long can Winter be your host.

So soon from virile dirt you will rise up
  From this prolific earth to windy skies
And bring with you the long-stemmed buttercup
  With multicolored wings of butterflies.

—LINES FROM *"Spring World, Awake"*
BY JESSE STUART

# Spring

Sound the flute!
Now it's mute.
Birds delight
Day and Night;
Nightingale
In the dale,
Lark in sky,
Merrily,
Merrily, merrily, to welcome in the Year.

Little Boy,
Full of joy;
Little Girl,
Sweet and small;
Cock does crow,
So do you;
Merry voice,
Infant noise,
Merrily, merrily, to welcome in the Year.

Little Lamb
Here I am;
Come and lick
My white neck;
Let me pull
Your soft Wool;
Let me kiss
Your soft face;
Merrily, merrily, we welcome in the Year.

—WILLIAM BLAKE

# Ground Hog Sees His Shadow

Ground Hog, who lived in a hole at one end of the field called High-Mowing, was a surly man. He had a mean disposition and no friends. Wearing an unbrushed ragged suit, he took his lonely way among cornstalks and bean poles, his small sharp eyes wary and his long yellow teeth ready for gnawing vegetables. He bit into fruit and then left it spoiled on the ground. He never gave a thought to his family. In fact, if Ground Hog ever met one of his relatives he bared his ugly teeth and tried to get to the vegetables first. And whatever he ate turned into fat, which made it possible for him to live without meals all winter.

So when the corn was made into sheaves, when the vegetable gardens were gone to stubble and the frosts came, Ground Hog retreated to the far end of his deep hole and went to sleep. Curled up in an untidy ball, he snored and dreamed of bigger and better crops another year.

He had no friends, and he was afraid; afraid of guns; yes, and afraid of his shadow. If Ground Hog ever saw his shadow he tried to flee from it. Of course the shadow went everywhere with him, but when he was stealing he seldom saw it, being concerned only with his stomach. But now in February, when there was an occasional day of sunshine and the warmth penetrated within Ground Hog's earth bed, he would stir, yawn, feel of his empty stomach, then crawl over to his doorway and peer out.

Now in February, there was an unexpected thaw. The sun rose earlier and set later above Temple Mountain and shone strong upon the orchard. Ground Hog poked his nose out of his hole and could scarcely believe his eyes. Drip, drip, came the melting drops from the icy boughs of the apple trees. He ventured out a little way, then farther. Like a giant with open mouth and long teeth right beside him on the snow, Ground Hog saw his shadow, larger and fiercer than last year. Not only did he see his shadow, but close beside stood a strange creature with a sharp nose, twig hands and feet, a rakish hat on the side of is hickory-nut head and a shrill voice.

"Halt!" said Miss Hickory, for it was she. Although she stood her ground, Miss Hickory too was scared. She had never seen Ground Hog before; and his teeth were close.

Ground Hog turned and ran into the depth of his hole. Miss Hickory ran, too, and did not stop until she fairly tumbled into the feathery, crooning midst of the huddled hen-pheasants, still living together in their Ladies' Aid Society in the shelter of the High-Mowing wall. The hens scattered, then rallied to her rescue as they covered her with their soft wings.

"There, there, my dear," Hen-Pheasant clucked. "You are among friends and safe, but whatever is the matter?"

When her breath came Miss Hickory told them. "I have just seen a wild animal! As large as the barn cat but with sharp yellow teeth! It was digging at the door of a hole with its shadow beside it."

"And then?" Hen-Pheasant looked anxious.

"It ran when it saw me, straight back into its hole."

"So you thought that Old Ground Hog ran from you!" Hen-Pheasant spoke firmly. "Ground Hog went back into his hole because he saw his shadow."

"And what of that?" Miss Hickory could scarcely believe her ears.

"Six weeks more of winter!" Hen-Pheasant moaned. "If Ground Hog comes out of his hole and the sun shines so that he sees his shadow, he goes back in again. For six weeks longer it snows, freezes, and blows."

"What makes him do that? I find my shadow, on a night when the moon is high, very pleasant company."

"Because Ground Hog is afraid. He steals vegetables, and he fancies his shadow will catch him. He keeps in the shade, away from his shadow as much as he can."

Miss Hickory took up the conversation. "All thieves are afraid. Why does he steal? Because he is hungry! What would you do if the farmer did not leave dried corn for you here at your nest? Look at your pile of uneaten corn. And more will come tomorrow. You should know what your duty is in a case like this. Your duty is acting as a member of Ladies' Aid, not just looking after yourselves like a lot of pigs."

"You mean that we should give away our corn?"

"And why not? Show Ground Hog a little neighborliness, and perhaps he will return the deed."

For a time there was silence among the hen-pheasants. It had not occurred to them to do more than take care of themselves. Although deserted by their cocks they had found sanctuary there in High-Mowing, and had been given food regularly. "Come again another day. Give us time to think," they told Miss Hickory.

But the next day the icy wind kept Miss Hickory home. Then

there were several days of thick fog. The sun did not shine for two weeks, but on a cloudy day Miss Hickory went once more to the Ladies' Aid Society. As soon as they saw her they began clucking, arguing among themselves.

"Hush up!" she told them. "This is no time to think of yourselves. Winter has lasted long enough, and if anything we can do will break it, let us do it." She filled both hands with yellow kernels of dried corn from the hen-pheasants' pile. "Come on!" she ordered.

Each timid hen took a kernel of corn in her bill; their President leading, they walked in line behind Miss Hickory until they came to the place where Ground Hog slept. They knew it was his hole, for they could hear his deep and regular snores.

"Spread the corn in front of his door," Miss Hickory told them. "Then run!"

They laid a square meal of corn in front of Ground Hog's hole. Miss Hickory rapped loudly on the door, and they all scattered, but watched from a safe distance. Ground Hog's snores subsided. He stirred, unrolled himself, and they saw his homely face with shifty black eyes peer cautiously out. Then he came entirely out and pounced upon the corn, eating greedily. He looked hither and yon, and since it was a dark day he saw no shadow. He closed his door and walked warily away from his hole, gnawing at the greening bushes that were pushing through the snow.

"Spring is coming!" Miss Hickory exclaimed.

"Spring is coming!" the hen-pheasants chorused.

—FROM *Miss Hickory* BY CAROLYN SHERWIN BAILEY

# The Snowdrop

The snow lay deep, for it was wintertime. The winter winds blew cold, but there was one house where all was snug and warm. And in the house lay a little flower; in its bulb it lay, under the earth and snow.

One day the rain fell, and it trickled through the ice and snow down into the ground. And presently a sunbeam, pointed and slender, pierced down through the earth, and tapped on the bulb.

"Come in," said the flower.

"I can't do that," said the sunbeam; "I'm not strong enough to lift the latch. I shall be stronger when springtime comes."

"When will it be spring?" asked the flower of every little sunbeam that rapped on its door. But for a long time it was winter. The ground was still covered with snow, and every night there was ice in the water. The flower grew quite tired of waiting.

"How long it is!" it said. "I feel quite cramped. I must stretch myself and rise up a little. I must lift the latch, and look out, and say 'good-morning' to the spring."

So the flower pushed and pushed. The walls were softened by the rain and warmed by the little sunbeams, so the flower shot up

31

from under the snow, with a pale green bud on its stalk and some long narrow leaves on either side. It was biting cold.

"You are a little too early," said the wind and the weather; but every sunbeam sang, "Welcome"; and the flower raised its head from the snow and unfolded itself—pure and white, and decked with green stripes.

It was weather to freeze it to pieces—such a delicate little flower—but it was stronger than anyone knew. It stood in its white dress in the white snow, bowing its head when the snowflakes fell, and raising it again to smile at the sunbeams, and every day it grew sweeter.

"Oh!" shouted the children, as they ran into the garden, "See the snowdrop! There it stands so pretty, so beautiful—the first, the only one!"

—HANS CHRISTIAN ANDERSEN (adapted)

# Shackles of Frost
## from Prehistoric Finland

Many, many years ago there came out of the North, from the dread land of Pohjola, a white spirit around whose thin shoulders was strapped a cold length of far-streaming fog. He was Kuljus, the frost spirit, at whose coming men shivered as with fear and the earth stiffened as in death.

From the spring maiden alone, who followed the horses of the sun in the long, white furrows of the skies, did Kuljus turn and flee, for she alone held the long, hot willow wand at whose touch the strength of the frost spirit melted away like mist at the the rising of the sun.

Far on the eastern edge of the land, where the sea came racing to the shore like fast steeds harnessed to purple sleighs, was the shop of Ilmarinen, the mighty smith. To his forge came daily the horses of the sun for bright new shoes with which to climb the slippery dome of ice that went up and over the earth like a pale blue bowl.

For weeks Kuljus, the frost spirit, hung on the edge of dark Pohjola, watching and waiting for his chance to enslave the earth.

33

At last, in the dead of night, he slipped down over the fields, and across the rivers with a blanket of gray mist woven of the spirits of frozen things. The blanket was as wide and heavy and thick as the deep sea.

With a wild shout, Kuljus seized this blanket by the corners and hung it from the pegs of the bright stars till it shut off from earth the pathway of the sun. Then weird, wild screams went under the eaves of the houses. Gusty breaths blew down the throats of the chimneys, scattering the fires. Kuljus was abroad going boldly over the land. He crawled behind fences. Near gates he whirled himself about. Through bushes he rustled his cold feet. He bit off the leaves of the trees, and imprisoned the springs and the streams with shackles of silvery ice. He crept up to the windowpanes and breathed silvery dreams over them, and he wove beautiful laces from the mist of the waterfalls.

To the forge of the great smith Ilmarinen came in the early dawn a little yellow wren. Above the glowing forge amid the black rafters it perched itself softly and preened its feathers with its brown beak.

"Ilmarinen," it said at last, "the horses of the spring maiden have lost their way. The blanket of Kuljus has hidden your forge from them. In vain do they scramble and plunge at the great slope beyond the dawn; in vain does the spring maiden lash them with long whips of light. Without shoes sharp from your anvil there will be no plowing done in the bright fields amid the stars."

Without making answer Ilmarinen laid his heavy, dark hand on the ram's-horn handle of the bellows and quickened the glow in the heart of the forge to a vivid white heat. Up and down went the handle of the blower, and hotter and hotter became the smithy until Kuljus, peering in at the cobwebby window, frowned at what he saw. Softly he laid his icy hands over the roof. His long, knotted fingers hung down over the low eaves in icicles almost to the ground.

Faster and faster went the forge—hotter and hotter grew the roof, until the fingers of Kuljus fell away from his hands and dropped with a dry rattle on the earth beneath. Then the corners of the blanket of fog were loosened from the stars and the blue sky shone through.

"Go now," cried Ilmarinen to the little yellow wren. "Fly away to the east and tell the spring maiden to drive hither the horses of the sun."

Then all the people were glad once more and crept out of their houses and pointed to the blue sky which became brighter and brighter as the horses of the sun came upward over the land's end.

"Clang! Clang!" went the hammers of the great smith, and the blaze of the white-hot iron filled the east with wonderful sparks that smote Kuljus, the frost spirit, like silver spears. Reeling, he fell backward toward the north, gathering about him his blanket of fog.

Then the horses of the sun, newly shod and strong, went swiftly up the fields of the sky, leaving a wide furrow of cloud turned over for the seeds of the spring maiden. Right gladly came she behind, scattering as she ran the seeds that flowered under her feet into the garden of the rainbow. Ever and anon some of the precious seed was wafted out of the furrow by the wind, to fall down on the earth to flower beside rocks, on hillsides, and in the gardens of men.

So Kuljus was beaten for the time, and Ilmarinen beholding the rainbow smiled, and the little yellow wren broken out into a sweet song that fluttered up to the ears of the spring maiden where she sowed flowers in the furrow of the horses of the sun.

—FROM *New Found Tales from Many Lands*

BY JOSEPH BURKE EGAN

# Ides of March

The new-leafed birch beside the river dreams;
May applēs spring from loam on tender stems.

Lean, hungry cattle prowl on greening hill
Searching for bullgrass and the daffodil.

The sun has thawed the winter's sleeping snake,
And one might be on any path you take.

Before the white-oak blossoms burst in full
Sheep have grown restless in their winter wool.

The cows steal out to calve in alder brush
Always so near a nest of singing thrush.

But slopes are filled with poke and turnip greens,
Potatoes gone and leather britches beans.

Potatoes pop up through the loamy mould
And sawbriers strut their leaves of windy gold.

Go to the yard and chase away the ox,
He's broken through to get the hollyhocks.

It's time the cattle should have exercise,
March wind is soothing to their winter eyes.

Foxes connive to show the hounds some speed,
Chickens to catch and little mouths to feed.

Welcome just anytime, conniving fox,
Five hound dogs snore behind the stovewood box.

How pleasant is the sun in heaven's arch
But earth is restless on the Ides of March.

—JESSE STUART

Jesse Stuart, who has traveled far and wide, grew up in the hills of Kentucky. After a serious illness, which he barely survived, he saw spring and his beloved hills with new appreciation. He shared his thoughts with all of us in a book called *The Year of My Rebirth:*

# Spring Comes to the Kentucky Hills

## March

Before I got out of bed, I heard them calling. Naomi has always contended one says "Phoebe," but I maintain he says "Pewee." Our annual visitors were back to build their nest, and this was exceedingly early for flycatchers. I wondered where they'd get enough insects to sustain life.

It was good to hear their calling. Theirs were the voices of old friends. I got up and looked out the window. Daylight was breaking. And the peewees, though I couldn't see either one of them, were hopping in the vines. Their voices brought memories. In the little house where I lived until I was nine, a pair came each spring. My father used to say, "Must be time to plow the garden, our pewees are back."

Always we watch for the very first signs of spring. This morning Naomi and I walked down the lane while the warm winds blew and lightning cut across the darkened heavens. We were looking for places where we planned to set Easter lilies beside the road for next spring.

"Look here," I said. "First blossoms of spring!"

"Hazelnut blooms," Naomi said.

We had for many years gathered hazelnuts from these bushes beside our land road. I'd gathered hazelnuts from these bushes many times on my way to and from school. When Naomi and I were married and came here to live, she didn't know hazelnut blooms until I showed them to her on this bush, their soft yellow-green tassels, like spears on corn tassels, clinging to leafless little branches.

The grass now shows signs of life in our front yard. Our big weeping willow is about to leaf. Dark rain clouds scoot over the wind just barely above the leafless sleeping trees on the hilltops. High above, the lightning is splitting these dark clouds, thunder following from one ridgetop to another.

"It's a scary time," Naomi said.

I agree. And then I thought: I should mark every day we have thunder in March. It's an old saying, "Thunder in March, on a corresponding day in May we'll have frost."

For the first time in days, the surge of the streams is louder than the March winds. Shinglemill roars down the narrow channel between the rock walls, by the redbud and dogwood trees and leaps through the large tile under our house like a bullet through a rifle barrel. Water runs in thin sheets over the rocks on the bluff, in streams down valleys, in ravines, and in ditches.

In this season of flood, I've seen the last road from town jammed with boys leading cows, men and women carrying belongings, pictures, and clothing, fleeing from high waters and looking for a home. Everybody in the county who lives in a higher, unflooded section opens his home to the refugees, large houses absorbing as many as six or seven wandering families.

Only one road leading to Greenup was open this morning. The river rose to high level Sunday, Monday to a higher level. When the sun breaks through the clouds the river's surface appears to be almost on a level with the streets in Greenup. People came to me this morning to get two empty houses to live in. They got them. They asked for a tool shed on the farm to store household effects in. They got it. Fortunately, the highlands around Greenup are so extensive in comparison with the flooded areas that the people without homes are a mere trickle to be absorbed, housed, and fed.

My sister and brother-in-law's house has two extra families. The old Daugherty place has been taken over. The Collins' house has a family moved in. The narrow W-Hollow Road is filled with parked or slow-moving vehicles. Another major flood is here. But this one I can only watch from the sidelines.

Water crested two days ago and started slowly receding yesterday. In W-Hollow we've had only the beauty and none of the destruction. The beauty of rain and singing streams that leap down hills and run in silver ribbons when the sun pops through the clouds.

Young tender leaves have come to the weeping willow, and now its long, green fronds wave toward me and swish in the wind like delicate fingers. The red buds have burst on the maple trees, the primrose and daffodils have blossomed in our yard. Green, growing, tender grass in early spring is one of the most fascinating things in the world. Even a few days before the official beginning of spring the grass had made my yard so beautiful that the cattle have already broken through fences to get in.

One morning I looked across our garden to see white blossoms on the steep bluff under the tall gray poplars. Then I knew spring must be here. The percoon was in blossom, most beautiful of all wild flowers. The petals were white as snow, and they fluttered in the wind of March.

When I went to college I learned percoon was really named

bloodroot, but percoon was the name my mother, father, and grand-parents knew. I learned that the word percoon came from the Cherokee Indians of North Carolina. They called this flower, from whose roots they extracted red juices for their war paints, puccoon. White settlers corrupted this to percoon, and that was the name I loved and grew up with.

## April

There is not a month in the year as fascinating as April. It is a month of bud, blossom, and leaf, and the awakening of sleeping life. Trees that have been naked, dark, somber, and dreaming so long, awake and dress in soft robes of green. This is the month of percoon white upon the bluffs, the month of trailing arbutus, which likes to hug close to the rock cliffs, babytears, cinquefoil, violets, and whippoorwill flowers, of dogwood, redbud, wild plum, and the multicolored blooms on the wild crabapple trees that cover our hill slopes.

April is the month to plow the garden, plant seeds, test Nature at her work. I am glad to be alive in April.

I thank God that He granted my stay here
    To count the many songs in winds that blow,
When April's spring returns again this year
    I'll walk with Him where rivers rise and flow.

Back to my valley for the blooming spring,
    Back to my garden and the wild bird's song,
To shadow, sun, and multicolored wing,
    The land, God must believe, where I belong.
           —ADAPTED FROM *The Year of My Rebirth*
                BY JESSE STUART

# First Spring

I think that God tossed into Spring
A large handful of birds to sing,
As He, Himself, grew lyrical
Witnessing His miracle.

—ALICE BOYD STOCKDALE

# Lo, the Winter Is Past

For, lo, the winter is past, the rain is over and gone;
The flowers appear on the earth;
   the time of the singing of birds is come,
and the voice of the turtle is heard in our land.

—THE SONG OF SOLOMON 2:11,12

# When Early March Seems Middle May

When country roads begin to thaw
   In mottled spots of damp and dust,
And fences by the margin draw
   Along the frosty crust
Their graphic silhouettes, I say,
The Spring is coming round this way.

When suddenly some shadow-bird
   Goes wavering beneath the gaze,
And through the hedge the moan is heard
   Of kine that fain would graze
In grasses new, I smile and say,
The Spring is coming round this way.

When through the twigs the farmer tramps,
   And troughs are chunked beneath the trees,
And fragrant hints of sugar-camps
   Astray in every breeze,—
When early March seems middle May,
The Spring is coming round this way.
—FROM *The Best Loved Poems and Ballards*
   *of James Whitcomb Riley*

# Making Maple Sugar

In many places in the United States and Canada early spring is the time for making maple sugar and syrup. Whe⌐ the sun warms the sap in sugar maples and starts it running and the nights are cold, thousands of girls and boys and men and women go out into the snowy woods to tap the trees, gather the sap, and boil it down, so that its sweetness may be enjoyed all through the year.

In the time when Indians set up their wigwams near the lakes in Wisconsin and Minnesota, a Chippewa medicine man sang this song:

> Let us go into the sugar camp
> While the snow lies on the ground,
> Live in the birch-bark wigwam—
> All the children and the older folk—
> While the people are at work.
>
> Make a fire in the sugar lodge
> So that we may boil the sap.
> Bring all the wooden ladles,

Set the wooden trough for graining.
All the people are at work.

Cut a notch in the maple tree,
Set a pail on the ground below,
Soon the sap will be flowing,
From the tree it will be flowing—
All the people are at work.

In the snow see the rabbit tracks,
Hear the note of the chickadee,
We must not stop to follow them,
'Tis the season of the sugar camp.
All the people are at work.

Bring the sap from the maple trees,
Pour the sap in the iron pot.
See how it steams and bubbles.
May we have a little taste of it?
All the people are at work.

Pour the syrup in the graining trough,
Stir it slowly as it thicker grows,
Now it has changed to sugar,
We may eat it in a birchbark dish.
There is sugar for us all.

—COLLECTED AND PARAPHRASED IN
ENGLISH BY FRANCES DENSMORE

# Spring

When, after the Winter alarmin',
The Spring steps in so charmin',
  So smilin' an' arch,
  In the middle o' March,
With her hand St. Patrick's arm on.
—FROM *The Three Owls, Second Book,*
BY ANNE CARROLL MOORE

# The River Bank

The Mole had been working very hard all the morning, spring-cleaning his little home. First with brooms, then with dusters; then on ladders and steps and chairs, with a brush and a pail of white-wash; till he had dust in his throat and eyes, and splashes of white-wash all over his black fur, and an aching back and weary arms. Spring was moving in the air above and in the earth below and around him, penetrating even his dark and lowly little house with its spirit of divine discontent and longing. It was small wonder, then, that he suddenly flung down his brush on the floor, said "Bother!" and "O blow!" and also "Hang spring-cleaning!" and bolted out of the house without even waiting to put on his coat. Something up above was calling him imperiously, and he made for the steep little tunnel which answered in his case to the graveled carriage-drive owned by animals whose residences are nearer to the sun and air. So he scraped and scratched and scrabbled and scrooged, and then he scrooged again and scrabbled and scratched and scraped, working busily with his little paws and muttering to himself, "Up we go! Up we go!" till at last—pop!—his snout came out into the sunlight, and he found himself rolling in the warm grass of a great meadow.

49

"This is fine!" he said to himself. "This is better than whitewash-ing!" The sunshine struck hot on his fur, soft breezes caressed his heated brow, and after the seclusion of the cellarage he had lived in so long the carol of happy birds fell on his dulled hearing almost like a shout. Jumping off all his four legs at once, in the joy of living and the delight of spring without its cleaning, he pursued his way across the meadow till he reached the hedge on the further side.

"Hold up!" said an elderly rabbit at the gap. "Sixpence for the privilege of passing by the private road!" He was bowled over in an instant by the impatient and contemptuous Mole, who trotted along the side of the hedge chaffing the other rabbits as they peeped hur-riedly from their holes to see what the row was about. "Onion sauce! Onion sauce!" he remarked jeeringly, and was gone before they could think of a thoroughly satisfactory reply. Then they all started grumbling at each other, "How stupid you are! Why didn't you tell him—" "Well, why didn't you say—" "You might have reminded him—" and so on, in the usual way; but, of course, it was then much too late, as is always the case.

It all seemed too good to be true. Hither and thither through the meadows he rambled busily, along the hedgerows, across the copses, finding everywhere birds building, flowers budding, leaves thrusting—everything happy and progressive and occupied. And in-stead of having an uneasy conscience pricking him and whispering "Whitewash!" he somehow could only feel how jolly it was to be the only idle dog among all these busy citizens. After all, the best part of a holiday is perhaps not so much to be resting yourself, as to see all the other fellows busy working.

He thought his happiness was complete when, as he meandered aimlessly along, suddenly he stood by the edge of a full-fed river. Never in his life had he seen a river before—this sleek, sinuous, full-bodied animal, chasing and chuckling, gripping things with a gurgle and leaving them with a laugh, to fling itself on fresh playmates that shook themselves free, and were caught and held again. All was a-shake and a-shiver—glints and gleams and sparkles, rustle and swirl, chatter and bubble. The Mole was bewitched, entranced, fascinated. By the side of the river he trotted as one trots, when very small, by the side of a man who holds one spellbound by exciting stories; and when tired at last, he sat on the bank, while the river still chattered on to him, a babbling procession of the best stories in the world, sent from the heart of the earth to be told at last to the insatiable sea.

As he sat on the grass and looked across the river, a dark hole in the bank opposite, just above the water's edge, caught his eye, and dreamily he fell to considering what a nice snug dwelling-place it would make for an animal with few wants and fond of a bijou riverside residence, above flood level and remote from noise and dust. As he gazed, something bright and small seemed to twinkle down in the heart of it, vanished, then twinkled once more like a tiny star. But it could hardly be a star in such an unlikely situation; and it was too glittering and small for a glowworm. Then, as he looked, it winked at him, and so declared itself to be an eye; and a small face began to grow up gradually round it, like a small frame round a picture.

A little face with whiskers. A grave round face, with the same twinkle in its eye that had first attracted his notice. Small neat ears and thick silky hair.

It was the Water Rat!

Then the two animals stood and regarded each other cautiously.

"Hullo, Mole!" said the Water Rat.

"Hullo, Rat!" said the Mole.

"Would you like to come over?" inquired the Rat presently.

"Oh, its all very well to talk," said the Mole, rather pettishly, he being new to a river and riverside life and its ways.

The Rat said nothing, but stooped and unfastened a rope and hauled on it; then lightly stepped into a little boat which the Mole had not observed. It was painted blue outside and white within, and was just the size for two animals; and the Mole's whole heart went out to it at once, even though he did not yet fully understand its uses.

The Rat sculled smartly across and made fast. Then he held out his forepaw as the Mole stepped gingerly down. "Lean on that!" he said. "Now then, step lively!" and the Mole to his surprise and rapture found himself actually seated in the stern of a real boat.

"This has been a wonderful day!" said he, as the Rat shoved off and took to the sculls again. "Do you know, I've never been in a boat before in all my life."

—FROM *The Wind in the Willows* BY KENNETH GRAHAME

# Song

The year's at the spring
And day's at the morn;
Morning's at seven;
The hill-side's dew-pearled;
The lark's on the wing;
The snail's on the thorn;
God's in his heaven—
All's right with the world!
—FROM *"Pippa Passes"*
BY ROBERT BROWNING

# A Blackbird Suddenly

Heaven is in my hand, and I
Touched a heartbeat of the sky,
Hearing a blackbird cry.

Strange, beautiful, unquiet thing,
Lone flute of God, how can you sing
Winter to spring?

You have outdistanced every voice and word,
And given my spirit wings until it stirred
Like you—a bird.

—FROM *"Sunrise Trumpets"*
BY JOSEPH AUSLANDER

# The First Dandelion

Simple and fresh and fair from winter's close emerging,
As if no artifice of fashion, business, politics had ever been,
Forth from its sunny nook of sheltered grass—innocent, golden,
  calm as the dawn,
The spring's first dandelion shows its trustful face.

—WALT WHITMAN

A big turtle sat on the end of a log
Watching a tadpole turn into a frog.
—FROM *Rocket in My Pocket*
COMPILED BY CARL WITHERS

# The Coming of Spring

There's something in the air
That's new and sweet and rare—
A scent of summer things—
A whir as if of wings.

There's something, too, that's new
In the color of the blue
That's in the morning sky,
Before the sun is high.

And though on plain and hill
'Tis winter, winter still,
There's something seems to say
That winter's had its day.

And all this changing tint,
This whispering stir and hint
Of bud and bloom and wing,
Is the coming of the spring.

And tomorrow or today
The brooks will break away
From their icy, frozen sleep,
And run, and laugh, and leap.

And the next thing, in the woods,
The catkins in their hoods
Of fur and silk will stand,
A sturdy little band.

And the tassels soft and fine
Of hazel will entwine,
And the elder branches show
Their buds against the snow.

So, silently but swift,
Above the wintry drift,
The long days gain and gain,
Until on hill and plain,

Once more, and yet once more,
Returning as before,
We see the bloom of birth
Make young again the earth.

—NORA PERRY

# The Daffodils

I wandered lonely as a cloud
   That floats on high o'er vales and hills,
When all at once I saw a crowd,
   A host of golden daffodils,
Beside the lake, beneath the trees
Fluttering dancing in the breeze.

Continuous as the stars that shine
   And twinkle on the milky way,
They stretched in never-ending **line**
   Along the margin of a bay:
Ten thousand saw I at a glance,
Tossing their heads in sprightly dance.

The waves beside them danced, but they
   Out-did the sparkling waves in glee:
A poet could not but be gay
   In such a jocund company:
I gazed—and gazed—but little thought
What wealth the show to me had brought:

For oft, when on my couch I lie
   In vacant or in pensive mood,
They flash upon that inward eye
   Which is the bliss of solitude;
And then my heart with pleasure fills,
And dances with the daffodils.

—WILLIAM WORDSWORTH

# Lines from "To John Keats, Poet, at Spring Time"

Spring beats
Her tocsin call to those who love her,
And lo! the dogwood petals cover
Her breast with drifts of snow, and sleek
White gulls fly screaming to her, and hover
About her shoulders, and kiss her cheek,
While white and purple lilacs muster
A strength that bears them to a cluster
Of color and odor; for her sake
All things that slept are now awake.

—COUNTEE CULLEN

# Cactus Kingdom

When April charms the desert ways,
   she leaves a path in flowers
so gay and so exquisite that
   they jewel the Springtime hours.

But when you start to name them,
   all romance flies away
for if you want to label them,
   here's what you'll have to say. . . .

That one's a staghorn cholla
   and that's a prickly pear;
this pink one's a devil finger,
   that's hedgehog over there . . .

There's a jumping cholla, beavertail,
   saguaro . . . barrel, too,
but beauty flowers in spite of all
   that prickly names can do!

—LORRAINE BABBITT

# Spring in the Desert

On sand riverbanks mesquite trees
    droop their slender, lace-leafed branches,
Fill the lonely air with fragrance,
    as a beauty unconfessed,
Till the wild quail comes at sunset
    with her timorous plumed covey,
And the iris-throated pigeon coo above
    her hidden nest.

Every shrub  distills vague sweetness;
    every poorest leaf has gathered
Some rare breath to tell its gladness
    in a fitter way than speech;
Here the silken cactus blossoms flaunt
    their rose and gold and crimson,
And the proud zahuara lifts its pearl-carved
    crown from careless reach.

—SHARLOT M. HALL

# Tree Portraits

A palo verde
is sunlit laughter
when Spring walks
desert ways;

A pepper tree is
a lace mantilla
through which the
moonlight plays.

—LORRAINE BABBITT

# When Ocotillos Bloom

Now come the glowing hours—
The thorns are tipped with flowers
That sweep in crimson haste
Across an arid waste.

The magic of their bloom
Is like a darkened room,
Which fills with shining light
From candles gay and bright.

Exultantly they fling
Their splendor to the spring—
Then suddenly are gone
Like candles burned too long.

   —IRENE WELCH GRISSOM

# From an American Cowboy Ballad

Early in spring we round up the dogies,
    Mark 'em and brand 'em and bob off their tails;
Round up the horses, load up the chuck wagon,
    Then throw the dogies upon the old trail.

It's whooping and yelling and driving the dogies;
    Oh, how I wish you would all go on!
It's whooping and punching and "Go on, little dogies,
    For you know Wyoming will be your new home."

# The Hare and the Hedgehog

Early one Sunday morning, when the cowslips or paigles were showing their first honey-sweet buds in the meadows and the broom was in bloom, a hedgehog came to his little door to look out at the weather. He stood with arms akimbo, whistling a tune to himself—a tune no better and no worse than the tunes hedgehogs usually whistle to themselves on fine Sunday mornings. And as he whistled, the notion came into his head that, before turning in and while his wife was washing the children, he might take a little walk into the fields and see how his young nettles were getting on. For there was a tasty beetle lived among the nettles; and no nettles—no beetles.

Off he went, taking his own little private path into the field. And as he came stepping along around a bush of blackthorn, its blossoming now over and its leaves showing green, he met a hare; and the hare had come out to look at his spring cabbages.

The hedgehog smiled and bade him a polite "Good morning." But the hare, who felt himself a particularly fine sleek gentleman in this Sunday sunshine, merely sneered at his greeting.

"And how is it," he said, "*you* happen to be out so early?"

"I am taking a walk, sir," said the hedgehog.

"A walk!" sniffed the hare. "I should have thought you might use those bandy little legs of yours to far better purpose."

This angered the hedgehog, for as his legs were crooked by nature, he couldn't bear to have bad made worse by any talk about them.

"You seem to suppose, sir," he said, bristling all over, "that you can do more with your legs than I can with mine."

"Well perhaps," said the hare, airily.

"See here, then," said the hedgehog, his beady eyes fixed on the hare, "I say you *can't*. Start fair, and I'd beat you naught to ninepence. Ay, every time."

"A race, my dear Master Hedgehog!" said the hare, laying back his whiskers. "You must be beside yourself. It's *childish*. But still, what will you wager?"

"I'll lay a golden guinea to a bottle of brandy," said the hedgehog.

"Done!" said the hare. "Shake hands on it, and we'll start at once."

"Ay, but not quite so fast," said the hedgehog. "I have had no breakfast yet. But if you will be here in half an hour's time, so will I."

The hare agreed, and at once took a little frisky practice along the dewy green border of the field, while the hedgehog went shuffling home.

"He thinks a mighty deal of himself," thought the hedgehog on his way. "But we shall see what we *shall* see." When he reached home he bustled in and looking solemnly at his wife said:

"My dear, I have need of you. In all haste. Leave everything and follow me at once into the fields."

"Why, what's going on?" says she.

"Why," said her husband, "I have bet the hare a guinea to a

Bottle of Brandy that I'll beat him in a race, and you must come and see it."

"Heavens! Husband," Mrs. Hedgehog cried, "are you daft? Are you gone crazy? You! Run a race with a hare!"

"Hold your tongue, woman," said the hedgehog. "There are things simple brains cannot understand. Leave all this fussing and titivating. The children can dry themselves; and you come along at once with me." So they went together.

"Now," said the hedgehog, when they reached the ploughed field beyond the field which was sprouting with young green wheat, "listen to me, my dear. This is where the race is going to be. The hare is over there at the other end of the field. I am going to arrange that he shall start in that deep furrow, and I shall start in this. But as soon as I have scrambled along a few inches and he can't see me, I shall turn back. And what *you*, my dear, must do is this: When he comes out of his furrow *there*, you must be sitting puffing like a porpoise *here*. And when you see him, you will say, 'Ahah! so you've come at last?' Do you follow me, my dear?" At first Mrs. Hedgehog was a little nervous, but she smiled at her husband's cunning, and gladly agreed to do what he said.

The hedgehog then went back to where he had promised to meet the hare, and he said, "Here I am, you see; and very much the better sir, for a good breakfast."

"How shall we run," simpered the hare scornfully, "down or over; sideways, longways; three legs or altogether? It's all one to me."

"Well, to be honest with you," said the hedgehog, "let me say this. I have now and then watched you taking a gambol and disporting yourself with your friends in the evening, and a pretty runner you are. But you never keep straight. You all go round and round, and round and round, scampering now this way, now that and chasing one another's scuts as if you were crazy. And as often as not you run uphill! But you can't run *races* like that. You must keep straight; you must begin in one place, go steadily on, and end in another."

"I could have told you that," said the hare angrily.

"Very well then," said the hedgehog. "You shall keep to that furrow, and I'll keep to this."

And the hare, being a good deal quicker on his feet than he was in his wits, agreed.

"*One! Two! Three!—and Away!*" he shouted, and off he went like a little whirlwind up the field. But the hedgehog, after scuttling along a few paces, turned back and stayed quietly where he was.

When the hare came out of his furrow at the upper end of the field, the hedgehog's wife sat panting there as if she would never be able to recover her breath, and at sight of him she sighed out, "Ahah! sir, so you've come at last?"

The hare was utterly shocked. His ears trembled. His eyes bulged in his head. "You've run it! You've run it!" he cried in astonishment. For she being so exactly like her husband, he never for a moment doubted that her husband she actually was.

"Ay," said she, "but I was afraid you had gone lame."

"Lame!" said the hare, "lame! But there, what's one furrow? 'Every time' was what you said. We'll try again."

Away once more he went, and he had never run faster. Yet when he came out of his furrow at the bottom of the field, there was the hedgehog! And the hedgehog laughed, and said: "Ahah! So here you are again! At last!" At this the hare could hardly speak for rage.

"Not enough! not enough!" he said. "Three for luck! Again, again!"

"As often as you please, my dear friend," said the hedgehog. "It's the long run that really counts."

Again, and again, and yet again the hare raced up and down the long furrow of the field, and every time he reached the top, and every time he reached the bottom, there was the hedgehog, as he thought, with his mocking, "Ahah! So here you are again! At last!"

But at length the hare could run no more. He lay panting and speechless; he was dead beat. Stretched out there, limp on the grass, his fur bedraggled, his eyes dim, his legs quaking, it looked as if he might fetch his last breath at any moment.

So Mrs. Hedgehog went off to the hare's house to fetch the bottle of brandy; and, if it had not been the best brandy, the hare might never have run again.

News of the contest spread far and wide. From that day to this, never has there been a race to compare with it. And lucky it was for the hedgehog he had the good sense to marry a wife like himself, and not a weasel, or a wombat, or a whale!

—WALTER DE LA MARE

# The Canoe in the Rapids

Once in another time, François Ecrette was an adventurer in the woods. Every winter he went north with Sylvain Gagnon. They trapped foxes, beavers, minks, and any furred creature that would step into their traps.

When spring came and the ice in the river melted, the two men would load their furs into a canoe and paddle down the swift current to sell their winter's catch to the trader.

It was one such spring that François and Sylvain headed south with the finest catch they ever made. If only they could beat the other trappers to the trading post, they could make a fine bargain.

"A-ah, we will be rich men," said Sylvain, who already could hear the tintin of coins in his deep pockets.

"Yes," answered François, "if we get through the Devil's Jaws safely."

Nowhere on any of the rivers of Canada was there such a fearsome place. In the Devil's Jaws there were waterfalls that roared and whirlpools that spun a boat about like a dry leaf. It was as if the river fell into a panic itself when squeezed into the Devil's Jaws and tried to run away in every direction.

71

"That's true," said Sylvain, "but you are lucky to have me for a partner. Nowhere in all Canada is there such a skillful boatman as Sylvain Gagnon."

Sylvain drew the cold air in through his nose and puffed out his chest with it.

So François Ecrette felt safe and happy, even though the worst ordeal of the long trip was ahead of them.

They loaded the canoe with their bundles of furs and their provisions. For days they paddled down the river, singing gay songs to pass away the long hours.

One late afternoon they beached their boat on the bank and made for a clearing on the hill. They built a campfire, and François started to roast a young rabbit he had shot. He hung it over the coals by spearing it on a green willow branch.

"We must eat well," said Sylvain, "for we are close to the Devil's Jaws. We will need all our strength for that pull and push."

"But it will soon be dark," François reminded him. "Shouldn't we camp here all night so we can go through the rapids in daylight?"

"Pou, pou," laughed Sylvain, "What a scared rabbit you are! I can paddle at night as well as by day. I could shoot the Devil's Jaws with my eyes closed and a beaver riding on my paddle."

François rubbed his stubbly chin.

"My faith," he exclaimed. "I am the luckiest man in the world to have you for a partner, Sylvain Gagnon. I don't believe you have fear of anything."

As if to test the truth of this, an angry growl came from behind the bushes. Both men jumped to their feet, François seizing his rifle as he did so. The bushes broke open, and a big brown bear came through them. He walked slowly on all fours, shuffling from this paw to that paw, and from that paw to this paw. Straight toward the two trappers he came.

François lifted his rifle to his shoulder and took careful aim. He pulled the trigger. Plink! Nothing happened. There was no bullet in the rifle because it had been used on the rabbit.

The bear gave another angry growl. He rose on his hind legs and walked toward François, shuffling from this paw to that paw.

François dropped the gun and ran for his life. Already Sylvain Gagnon was far ahead of him, his fur coat making him look like a bear that ran too fast to shuffle from this paw to that paw. François made for a big tree, but he didn't have time to climb it as the bear was almost on him. So around the tree he ran. And behind him followed the bear. Round and round and round the tree ran François and the bear. Any little bird looking down from the treetop wouldn't have known whether the bear was chasing François Ecrette or François was chasing the bear. The trapper ran so fast that he was more behind the bear than in front of him. And as the bear ran around the tree, he clawed the air angrily. But his sharp claws only tore the bark from the tree. And if François had anything at all to be thankful for, it was that the ragged shreds flying through the air were bark from the tree and not skin from his back.

Around and around went the man and the beast. The bear got dizzy first. He ran slower and slower. Finally he broke away from the tree and went staggering away, first to this side and then to that side. And as he reeled and stumbled, he knocked his head into one tree trunk after another. Bump—bump—bump.

François lost no time in finding another tree to climb, for the tree they had been running around had been stripped of its bark as far up as a bear could reach. As he climbed, he could hear the bump, bump of the bear's head as he stumbled into tree trunks.

Panting and dizzy himself, François settled into a crotch of the tree. Now where was that false friend, Sylvain Gagnon, who had left him to face the bear alone? He called and called, but there was no answer. Perhaps the bear had eaten Sylvain. A-tout-tou, what bad luck that would be when there was still the Devil's Jaws ahead! How could he ever get through those treacherous waters without the skillful boatman Sylvain Gagnon?

And how could he get safely from the tree to the boat? Perhaps the bear was waiting for him among the bushes. The sleepy sun soon went to bed, and it grew dark. It became colder than ever. François Ecrette's arms and legs were numb.

At last he jerkily lowered himself from the tree. He looked about in every direction, but it was too dark to see anything. He sniffed and sniffed like a bear, for if a bear can smell a man, maybe a man can smell a bear. But all François could smell was the sharp, icy air of early spring. Slowly he made his way down the hill.

Then great joy filled the heart of François Ecrette. Although the trees blackened the river, a faint moonlight glimmered through them. Its pale light fell upon a figure hunched in the bow of the canoe with the fur coat pulled up over its ears.

"Sylvain," cried François, "you are safe after all. Why didn't you come back to me?"

But Sylvain must have felt a deep shame, for he only put his head down between his arms and made a sad, apologetic sound.

"Believe me, my friend," said François, "I'm certainly glad you escaped, for we have a terrible ride ahead of us this night. Do you think we better try the rapids after all?"

But his companion resolutely straightened up and squared his shoulders in the fur coat. François pushed the boat into the stream, leaped aboard and grabbed a paddle. Silently they floated into the current; then the slender canoe headed for the dangers ahead.

"My faith, it is good to have you in this boat with me," cried François. "This current is like a bolt of lightning."

The boat raced faster and faster. Instead of paddling for speed, François had to spend his strength flattening the paddle like a brake. The trees made a dark tunnel of the river course so that François could barely see his companion's stout back.

On, on they went. The frail canoe sped in a zigzag flight like a swallow. François Ecrette's sharp ear caught the distant roar of the rapids.

"Brace yourself, Sylvain," he cried, "for the boat is now in your hands. I will help as much as I can."

So he plied his paddle from this side to that side and from that side to this side. The river had become like an angry, writhing eel. He heard the waterfall ahead and began paddling like mad so the canoe would shoot straight and true. The least slant of the boat and the churning current would turn it over and over, and swallow them both.

François felt the icy wind and the cold spray on his face as they plunged over the waterfall and bobbed in the whirlpool below. He fought the churning, frothing waters that he could hear more than see. His muscles tightened like iron and the air blew up his lungs.

"My faith, but it's a good thing to have such a boatman as Sylvain Gagnon guiding this canoe," rejoiced François. "In such a current as this, no other man could bring a boat through safely. I will forget the way he deserted me when the big brown bear attacked us."

All danger was not over yet, for the stern of the canoe was sucked into the outer rim of a whirlpool. The lurch of the boat wrenched François Ecrette's back like a blow from a giant hammer.

The canoe spun around completely. For fully ten minutes, there was such a battle with the churning waters as François had never known before. Around and around, up and down rocked the canoe, with François fiercely wielding his paddle. If it hadn't been for the soothing figure in front of him, he would have given up in fright.

Finally the canoe straightened out and leaped straight ahead. The roar of the rapids grew fainter. François let his paddle drag.

"My faith," he gasped. "I thought that was the last of us for sure. You have saved us both, Sylvain Gagnon. No boatman in all Canada but you could have gotten us out of that Devil's trap."

But his modest companion only shrugged his shoulders and humped lower into the bow.

Then because François was worn out from his paddling, he decided to take a little nap. With no other partner but Sylvain would he have dared doze off. But Sylvain had proved his mettle in getting them through the rapids, and the waters ahead were slow and peaceful. So François rested his paddle, closed his eyes, and fell asleep.

When he awoke, it was morning. The sun had chased the shadows out from under the trees, and the river sparkled in the friendliest kind of way.

François rubbed the sleep out of his eyes.

"Ah, Sylvain," he yawned, "what a night we had in the rapids. If it hadn't been for you—a-tou-tou-tou-tou!"

For François Ecrette's partner in the canoe was not Sylvain Gagnon, the great boatman, but the big brown bear of the clearing!

François jumped up and gave a bloodcurdling shriek. The bear slowly turned around and looked at him. He shook his great furry head as if to shake his brains back into their right place after they had been knocked apart by the tree trunks. He gave a low threatening growl.

François didn't wait any longer. He dived into the river and furiously swam through the icy water. After what seemed to be a sinner's lifetime, he reached the frosty shore. When he looked back at the river, he had a last glance of the canoe, full of furs, disappearing among the trees with the big brown bear standing in the bow.

Now this was a fine how-does-it-make of trouble. Here was François all alone in the wilderness, without Sylvain, fur, provisions, or even a dry match.

Luckily the trading post couldn't be too far away now. François gathered dry wood and started a fire in the Indian way, by rubbing two sticks together. Then he stood as close to the fire as he could, to dry out his clothes. He scorched and steamed like the uneaten rabbit back on the sharp stick in the clearing.

At last he was dry enough to brave the cold walk down the river bank. He set out slowly. The branches scratched his hands and face. His boots sloshed and squashed through the slush of early spring.

It was late afternoon by the time he reached the trader's village. Everyone seemed surprised to see him alive.

"Your canoe was found caught in a log jam below here, with bear tracks on the shore," said the trader. "We thought a bear had carried you off."

"But the furs," cried François. "What happened to them? Were they lost?"

"They are all safe," said the trader. "Your friend Sylvain Gagnon arrived only a little while ago. He helped me check through them."

Then a familiar face appeared in the crowd.

"François, my good friend," cried Sylvain. "I got a ride back with a party of Indians. But how did you ever get the canoe through the rapids all by yourself?"

"Sylvain, my false friend," retorted the trapper, "I was not alone. The big brown bear who chased me in the clearing was with me."

Then François Ecrette shivered and shook in a way that had nothing to do with the cold spring afternoon or his damp clothing.

So all turned out well for François Ecrette in the end. But he never went on any more trapping trips with Sylvain Gagnon. You see, my friends, one who turns into a big brown bear when you need him most is not a true friend.

—NATALIE SAVAGE CARLSON

# Spring Grass

Spring grass, there is a dance to be danced for you.
Come up, spring grass, if only for young feet.
Come up, spring grass, young feet ask you.

Smell of the young spring grass,
You're a mascot riding on the wind horses.
You came to my nose and spiffed me. This is your lucky year.

Young spring grass just after the winter,
Shoots of the big green whisper of the year,
Come up, if only for young feet.
Come up, young feet ask you.

—CARL SANDBURG

# The First Lamb

His name was Abd el Karuzeh, and both his father and mother pronounced it down in their throats so that each syllable sounded almost the same as all the others, like the echo of pebbles dropped into a deep well. It was a big name for a small boy, but his size was deceiving. He was older than he looked. None of the men and women who make their homes in the limestone caves in southern Algeria, in that low range of hills which separates the coastal plain from the desert, are big people.

Abd el Karuzeh was ten years old, and for two years now he had helped herd the village flocks. Every morning he and the other boys of his age went from cave to cave and called out the sheep and goats of the family or families living within. Then uphill they all trooped, following trails which only familiar eyes could recognize and scaling slopes which only sheep, goats, and boys bred to mountains could climb.

One by one, Abd el Karuzeh and the other boys rounded up out of the flock a dozen or so ewes with their lambs and stopped on some slope where the African sun had coaxed a faint tinge of green out of the jutting rocks and sour soil. Sheep were stupid creatures,

Abd el Karuzeh's father said, and there had to be an abundance of food under their very noses—else they would starve to death! Farther on, where only weeds and thistles struggled against the rocks, the older boys pastured the goats. While beyond even that, among the crags where human eyes could discover almost no green thing, the boys who were no longer children but not yet men foraged along with the tribe's camels for a precarious existence. They did not return to the caves at night, but lived and slept with their grumbling, ungainly charges for months at a time. Therefore, each of them carried a spear, for no one knew when a lion would spring from a rock.

Abd el Karuzeh carried a dagger stuck through his belt, but lions seldom came close to the caves. He had only hyenas to fear— and then only after dark. Darkness comes quickly in the mountains once the sun has set. And well he knew that when shadows to the east of the rocks began to grow blue, he must gather his ewes and their lambs together and hurry down the hill. The patter of hooves on the rocks was a dainty and light sound, but a hyena made no sound at all until its powerful jaws snapped through a lamb's neck.

The old men of the tribe said a hyena could follow a man unnoticed until its hot breath scorched his heels. There were evil spirits, Abd el Karuzeh had heard from these men, which lived among the rocks and roamed the hills at night. Sometimes they took the form of a hyena and followed travelers. Whenever one rose up onto its hind legs and whispered into a man's ear, that man spoke only foolishness from then on and became a burden to his tribe, said the old men.

But Abd el Karuzeh was not thinking of hyenas or foolish men one particularly sunny spring afternoon. He was swinging his bare legs over the edge of a huge rock and pitying himself a lot. His father was poor, to begin with. Poor, even for the cave dwellers of southern Algeria. He owned only a half dozen sheep, and he had not, like other fathers, given his son a lamb with which to start a flock of his own.

"You must earn your first lamb," he had replied shortly to Abd el Karuzeh's pleading. But he turned his face away when he said it, for Abd el Karuzeh's father loved his son, and it was hard to deny him this thing.

Like all fathers he dreamed of the day when he would sit among the old men and listen to Abd el Karuzeh, then become a grown man, help direct the tribal council. But like all fathers he also knew that if Abd el Karuzeh did not own flocks of sheep and goats and camels, no one would listen to him. Poor men can be as good as rich men, but no one asks their advice. And how was any boy to start a flock without even one lamb to call his very own? So Abd el Karuzeh's father could not meet his son's eyes as he had replied, "You must earn your first lamb!"

So the boy sat perched on a big rock and dangled his legs down its warm sides as he wrestled with his problem. What could he do to earn a lamb? He asked himself the question a thousand times, but there was no answer. The only way Abd el Karuzeh had ever known a boy to get a lamb was for his father to give it to him. If his father was too poor—

Abd el Karuzeh did not like the thought. So he banged his bare calloused heels against the rocks and squinted across the valley at the cliff ten miles away. He knew that above and below that cliff other boys were herding sheep and goats. Almost every one of those boys could look at his flock and point out a lamb, or perhaps a ewe and her lamb that belonged to him!

Abd el Karuzeh knew they loved their sheep. That when the anemones and cyclamen splashed color over the hills after the rainy season, they wove wreaths for their sheep's necks and tied bouquets to their legs and fat tails. That on frosty nights when the fires died down and the heat had gone out of the caves, they crept among the animals in the corner and snuggled up to their own sheep for warmth.

But what could a boy do to earn a lamb? Even a sickly lamb? Or a crippled lamb? If he could kill a lion or a leopard and bring the skin to the Headman, then the tribe would give him almost anything—a sheep, a goat, even a camel! But Abd el Karuzeh knew that not many grown men had killed a leopard, and even fewer had killed a lion. No, he would have to think of some other way.

What could he do? And when could he do it? He arose every morning before the sun had cleared all the mist away from the cave entrance, took the bit of bread and cheese his mother gave him, and set off for the hills with the other shepherds. There he kept one eye out for eagles which might carry off a lamb that had strayed too far from its mother, and watched with the other for any small animal he might kill with a rock and roast over a little fire of thorns for his midday meal.

A shout aroused Abd el Karuzeh, and he looked up to greet another shepherd. The sun was already red in the western sky, and shepherds were rounding up their flocks to return to the caves. Abd el Karuzeh, being one of the youngest boys, did not go so far into the hills as the others, so he waited as they brought up their sheep. The sun sank lower and lower, and the crags to the west pierced its red disk.

"Fuad and Feragi are late," one shepherd murmured uneasily, looking at the blue shadows already stealing across the lowest rocks.

"Do you see them anywhere, Abd el Karuzeh?" asked another. "Your eyes are sharp."

Abd el Karuzeh scanned the slopes, but there was no sign of the two boys and their flock. The uneasiness among the boys grew. Fuad and Feragi were brothers and sons of the Headman, but the boys would have waited for their poorest comrade. No shepherd deserts a fellow shepherd in the hills at night. For the hyena, which is a skulking coward under the sun, is feared by grown men under the stars. Where were Fuad and Feragi? Even the sheep and goats bunched together as though afraid.

But what was that? It sounded like the patter of raindrops on dry leaves. A sigh of relief broke from the boys, and even the flock started milling about as though glad. Hurrying down the pathway came the Headman's sons and their sheep. But they were not happy boys.

"We have had to abandon a lamb," said Fuad, the elder.

Relief among the boys changed to dismay. Not only are his charges wealth to a shepherd; he loves them as a mother loves the baby that depends upon her helplessly. And just as no mother will desert her baby, neither will a good shepherd desert one of his flock.

"What happened?" someone asked in a low voice, and every boy strained forward listening.

Feragi pointed to a big white ewe that kept sniffing the lambs of the flock and bleating softly now and then. She was hunting for a lamb which was not there!

"She-of-the-Nimble-Toes strayed off a bit from the flock," he said, "and I went after to bring her back. When I was but several steps from her, I saw an adder among the stones between us, and I threw a rock at it. I crushed the poisonous snake's head, but our ewe, She-of-the-Nimble-Toes, was frightened and leaped sideways, knocking her lamb over the cliff."

"Could you not reach it?" Abd el Karuzeh knew the answer before he asked.

"No," Fuad replied. "It fell on a small ledge and if we could have gotten down to it, we could not have climbed back up again. It is a pity, too, for She-of-the-Nimble-Toes comes of good stock, and her lambs make fine sheep.

"And it was unhurt," Feragi put in.

"It will not remain unhurt long," Fuad remarked shortly. "Even now a hyena or the jackals may have it. Oh, we tried to get it, of course, but the rock was brittle and snapped under our hands, and the bushes broke under our weight. We were too big and heavy."

"I thought Fuad was going to fall once," Feragi interrupted.

"And you dangled your cloak over the cliff for me to hold on to—and risked being pulled over after me. Didn't you? You are a brave, good brother!"

"I'd rather have you than a lamb any day," Feragi grinned, although he was embarrassed by his brother's praise.

"Well, you have me. But it is late, and we must get the rest of the flock back to the caves before we lose any more," Fuad replied as he started his companions and the animals down the trail.

A lamb, a fine lamb, alive and unhurt on a ledge where he might rescue it. Back there, too, there might be jackals or hyenas ready to devour either lamb or boy!

"Yah hya ris!" came the chorus of the shepherds' song. That way lay food, fires, companionship, safety. As Abd el Karuzeh looked after the boys, he saw Fuad stride over to a tired lamb, pick it up, and swing its soft body around his neck like a collar. Fuad was a good shepherd. He would never have deserted a lamb if it had been at all possible for him to rescue it.

With sudden determination, Abd el Karuzeh turned and trotted off into the darkness. One by one the stars pierced the Algerian sky, and the moon swam in a faint azure glow.

Abd-el Karuzeh found himself singing under his breath as he hurried along. When he thought of the words of the song he could not think of what might lurk in the shadows. And when he sang even faintly, he could not hear what might creep up behind him.

A stone rolled down the hillside, and he began to run in terror. Was there really anything following him? He clasped his hands over his ears so he could hear no evil. He had no desire to go through life talking foolishness! On and on he sped, his heart in his throat and his pulse pounding in his ears.

His foot dashed another stone downhill, and his pulse struck a new note. Or was it his pulse? He jerked his hands from his ears and listened.

Baaaaaaah!

Only a lamb—a cold lamb—bleated like that!

Ba-a-a-a-a-a-h!

He followed the quavering sound. Here was the cliff. Here was a clean space where Fuad's and Feragi's bodies had brushed all the dirt and stones aside as they tried to worm their way down the cliff. And there, looking up at him, from below, was She-of-the-Nimble-Toes' lamb!

Abd el Karuzeh took off his cloak, slid on his stomach over the cliff, and with his toes felt for a bit of jutting rock. Almost inch by inch the boy descended, his body plastered to the rock in front of him, his skin wet with sweat from exertion and the nervous strain. Time after time as he eased his weight from one foot to the other the rock crumbled and went crashing down the mountainside. Only his strong fingers saved him. Fuad had been right. The shrubs were too small and the rock too brittle and crumbly to have held a larger boy.

At last he stood on the ledge beside the lamb. He picked it up, and it nuzzled its head against his chest. As he stroked its warm wool, he could see in the pale moonlight that there were stains on its back, and he saw, too, that his fingers were bleeding.

Blood has a very strong odor to animals. Abd el Karuzeh cowered back against the cliff and peered to the right and left of him. There was no time to waste. The smell of blood would surely bring animals, and quickly. He slung the lamb about his neck as he had seen Fuad do, took off his belt, and tied its feet together.

Climbing down the cliff had been slow, hard work. Climbing up was even slower and more difficult. He was tired. His fingers hurt. The lamb about his neck made him feel awkward and off balance. Its feet scraped the rock. He could not plaster his face as close to the cliff as he wanted to—as he knew was safe! If the lamb grew nervous and kicked, even a little bit, it might plunge them both into the abyss below. There might be a hyena jumping for his feet—or one waiting for him above. His pulse pounded in his ears so loudly he could hear nothing.

It seemed an eternity before his hands had struck a broad expanse of level rock and he had wormed his thin little belly over the top of the cliff. To safety?

Abd el Karuzeh was not quite sure how far he was from his father's cave. He looked down the long pathway he must cover, and his breath caught in his throat. A gleam of light! Was it a hyena's eyes? Now many gleams! A pack of jackals?

Then he laughed aloud—animals' eyes are in pairs, and they are steady in the darkness. These lights bobbed up and down singly. Too, animals tread softly, and Abd el Karuzeh's keen ears caught the sound of footsteps almost as soon as he had seen the torches.

"Saiida," he shouted, pulling the second syllable out into a long high-pitched note: e-e-e-e-e-e-e-!

"Hallo-o-o-o-o-o-o-o!" came back his father's voice before his own echoes had died away. The rocks rattled beneath his feet as he sped down the path; but there was no need to slip along quietly now. No animal, however hungry or fierce, attacks a party of men with fire in their hands.

Fuad and Feragi were in the group, and their father. Abd el Karuzeh untied the lamb and placed it in Fuad's hands.

"Why do you do that, Abd el Karuzeh?" the Headman asked.

"Did not your sons tell you?" Abd el Karuzeh asked in surprise. "It belongs to you. It is the lamb of your ewe, the one we shepherds call She-of-the-Nimble-Toes."

"It is a lamb my sons abandoned to die," the Headman replied slowly, "therefore, it no longer belongs to anyone in my family. We could not wear its wool with satisfaction. We could not claim its lambs with honor.

"Fuad," the Headman turned to his son, "return the lamb to its rightful owner!"

Tears slid from Abd el Karuzeh's eyes and sank into the lamb's soft wool. It was not manly to cry, he knew; but now not only his fingers throbbed—but his heart was very full.

"Abd el Karuzeh!" His father spoke sharply as poor men the world over are apt to do when they are very proud of their children. The boy sank on one knee before the Headman and laid his forehead upon the palm of the Headman's hand in sign of thanks and tribal submission.

Then, with Fuad on one side and Feragi on the other, and his lamb—his very own lamb—cradled in his arms, Abd el Karuzeh followed the men back to the safety, warmth, and companionship of the caves.

—LOUISE A. STINETORF

# Yo Han and the Baby Camel

The Camel Inn was very still in the late afternoon light. Mud brick walls topped by thorns surrounded the court, in which were kneeling sixty or more camels. They were great Bactrians, whose beady eyes stared in an unfriendly fashion. Not a leaf showed on the old willow tree, but the March sun warmed the earth.

With a little sound the great wooden gate opened a crack, and a small boy slipped through. He kept in the shadow of the gate and looked about the inn yard for a place to hide. One of the camel packs stood near him. On each side of the wooden pack frame was a great basket made for carrying coal. This one was empty.

The boy climbed into the empty basket nearest him, and pulled an old sheepskin over the top to cover it completely. Fu Shung and Gin Bao, with whom he was playing hide-and-seek, would never find him here. Now he heard their shrill voices over the mud wall. "Yo Han! Yo Han! Where has he hidden?"

"Come on, Fu Shung, he must have gone into the old Peony Temple yard," called another voice. The voices became fainter. Then all was quiet except for the crunching of the camels as they chewed their cuds.

91

Yo Han, or Johnny, as his parents called him, was an American boy with fair hair and slate gray eyes. He had often wished to have black hair and eyes like all his friends. At least, they were kind about it, and said he was just as much fun as if he were Chinese.

Now he wondered how long it would be before one of the boys would find him. This was the very best hiding place he had ever found, but it was hot and smelled rather strong of camel. The slanting sunshine made patterns on his hands and arms as it shone through the woven sides of the basket. He wondered how soon these camels would be going to Mongolia to their summer feeding grounds. Soothed by the drone of flies and thoughts of far Mongolian plains, he went to sleep.

At dusk the camel drivers came out of the dark little inn room where they slept out the day. Sitting on their heels in the courtyard, they had their bowl of millet cereal and a couple of flat biscuits before the job of loading began.

"How is the baby camel?" a driver called to Lao Wang, an old man in a patched jacket who owned ten of the camels.

"The little one is strong enough, but it has a soreness in the eyes. I am afraid it will be blind. Then what use will it be to me? Misfortune is always my lot," sighed Lao Wang, as he got up to arrange his loads. The mother camel was the finest in his string. She brought up the end of the line and carried on her neck the great bell, which Lao Wang, riding on the first camel, could hear— "cling, clang"—all night long. This told him that all was well; no one of the beasts had broken his rope or strayed.

The baby camel was to ride on one side of his mother's load. The old man peered at the other basket; it was already loaded, and a sheepskin thrown over the top. When the squealing little camel had been pushed into his basket, his long awkward legs folded under him, Lao Wang called one of the men to help him. They lifted the pannier frame onto the old camel's back, as she knelt munching her cud and twitching her delicate nose, first this way, then that.

"Ai-ho! Up we go!" the men called as they hoisted the pack strongly into place. A jerk at the nose rope gave the old camel her signal to rise. First her back legs unfolded slowly, then her front. The pack from which the baby camel's head stuck out rose up until it was six feet in the air.

The little camel craned his neck to look down. He could not see the ground and called his mother, "Maa-a-a-a." From the twilight ahead came his mother's reassuring voice, "Moo-oo."

The drivers called "Di-di-di-hooo!"

The camel train wound out of the inn yard, each camel's nose rope fastened onto the pack of the beast ahead. On the lead camel a man rode, swaying high between the two great humps. The camels' great padded feet sank into the fine dust, which came up "puff, puff," between their spreading toes.

Camels have their own inns and may travel only at night, for mules cannot abide their smell. Lines of pack mules, mule-drawn carts, and carriages crowd the roads in the daytime; and all night long under the stars the camels pad along the brown North China roads.

Great stars lit up the sky. The outline of the city wall and a ghostly white pagoda rose dim as the camel caravan—one, ten, thirty, sixty camels—padded softly by. There was no sound but the low, full clang of the bell on every seventh camel's neck.

As they left the shadow of the city wall, the wind blew coldly down the sunken road. On each side rose high banks of loose earth, composed of fine, drifted particles deposited through the centuries by winds sweeping down from the Gobi Desert.

"Ma-a-a-a," bleated the baby camel. "Ma-a-a-a," the sound echoed back from the high banks bordering the road. "Moo-oo," answered the mother's deep voice.

The strange sound wakened a small boy who had slept very soundly, curled up in a great wicker basket. For a moment John thought he must be back on the Empress of Canada, the ship which had brought him back to China from a long visit to his grandmother the year before. The swaying motion was very like a ship, but when he pulled the old coat away and pushed his head out into the night air, great stars were burning above him, white and thick in a wide ribbon across the sky. The dark earth stretched out flat on either side. Across the camel's hump he could see something bobbing up and down—a little head with silky ears, squinting eyes, and a nose that snuffed delicately like a rabbit's.

Now John remembered how he had hidden in the big pannier in the courtyard of the camel inn. He must have been asleep when the men hoisted the pack onto the camel's back. But what was the little animal in the other basket? Could it really be a baby camel? Was the camel train on its way to Mongolia?

John hoped so. Winter evenings he often stood by his gate for as long as an hour watching the camel caravans go by in the dusk, the bells sounding sweet and clear. He knew the camels traveled every summer up to the wide grassy plains of Mongolia. There they would fatten on thorns and sagebrush which even the ponies and sheep could not eat, and store up fat in their humps for the long winter ahead. Flowers grow everywhere there, and there are miles and miles of grasslands with only herds of Mongol ponies, sheep, and antelope, and here and there a Mongol yurt like an overgrown bee-hive along the edge of the sky.

John was not a bit afraid. The night air was chilly, so he pulled the sheepskin about his shoulders and sniffed the beautiful smells of spring. The little camel's head, bobbing up and down, looked very soft. John reached out and touched it hesitantly. Then, finding the little beast was not afraid, he stroked it and fondled the little ears and felt along the curving neck and the tiny soft humps. It was like velvet all over. What fun to ride this way for days and days, beside a baby camel, watching all the world go by!

He slept again, to waken when the beginning of dawn had cast a pale green light behind the edge of the hills. The hills turned purple, then rose, with the reflected light of the sunrise. Fields beside the road showed green with winter wheat, and the willow trees by the roadside were orchid against the deep blue sky. A little town appeared ahead, a jumble of gray tile roofs and brick walls.

John yawned and stretched and knelt in the basket, holding firmly to the sides, and looked as far ahead as he could. The camel train was turning into a wide gateway. He huddled down again in the basket and pulled the coat over his head. What would the camel drivers do with a stowaway?

"Sook! Sook!" called Lao Wang at the camel's head, jerking the nose rope to make her kneel. The basket plunged forward, then back, and came to rest on the solid ground.

"Ma-a-a-a," bleated the little camel, hungry for his breakfast. John cautiously pushed aside the basket covering, and looked up into the wrinkled face of Lao Wang.

"Look, look!" called Lao Wang to the other drivers. "Look at what is in my bell camel's basket! A little boy, very strange, a little Western child with white hair like an old, old man!"

All the drivers clustered about in a circle. "Ai-yah! Ai-yah!" they exclaimed. "This has never happened to us before. A baby camel on one side of the load and a little foreign child on the other!"

"Where did you come from, little son?" asked Lao Wang. "Who is your venerable father, and how did you get into my camel pack?"

John explained who he was and where he lived and told them about the game of hide-and-seek. Lao Wang nodded solemnly. "I have heard good words of the doctor, your honorable father. In my own village a tree fell on a man and broke his leg. His two brothers carried him in a basket slung from a pole to the American hospital at Taiku. In a month he was back in my village, doing the work of a man. Yes, yes, your father, Hu Dai Fu, is a good man."

"But, I," interrupted John, "I would like to go to Mongolia with your camel train, kind driver."

Lao Wang's wrinkled face broke into a wide smile. His eyes quite hid away in the wrinkles, and he put his dark hand on the little boy's fair hair.

"So, the little American wants to go with Lao Wang to Mongolia. But let us see. Your father and mother do not know where you are. Even now they may think that men with bad hearts have taken the little son away to hold for ransom, or that the hungry gray wolf from the hills stole into the village and carried him away. Before we talk of far journeying, should we not let them know you are well and with friends?"

This aspect of the matter had not occurred to John before. His mother would be worried. He had never been away from his parents at night before. But how could he let them know?

"How far is it to the city of Taiku, where my father lives, Lao Wang?"

"We have traveled sixty li during the night, little son," replied Lao Wang. "This is about twenty miles. There are many rickshaw-pullers going back to Taiku this morning. We will find one to take a message back to the Hospital for Hu Dai Fu, your father."

At the gate, Lao Wang called to a rickshaw-puller to stop. The man had a light load and promised to run as fast as possible to the American doctor at Taiku and tell him of the safety and whereabouts of his son.

Inside the low, mud-brick building where the drivers stayed during the day, a brick bed, or kang, filled half the room. A low stove, also of brick, at one end of it, sent warm air under the bed, so that a thin quilt, even on the coldest day, would keep a man comfortable. But no one thought of sleeping yet. The camels had to be unloaded and fed and watered and bedded down for the day.

One of the drivers lit a fire under a great black iron pot. Then he measured millet from a sack and cut up a big yellow squash into cubes, and put all into the boiling water. To John's sniffing nose it smelled better than turkey with cranberry sauce. He had not known how hungry he was. When Lao Wang handed him a steaming bowl of it, and a great fried biscuit filled with chopped onions, he was perfectly content.

Each driver took his bowl and biscuit and squatted outside the door where the morning air was fresh, and each could watch his own camels dozing in the sun. The talk was men's talk, slow, with pauses for a pipe to be filled and smoked. Three long draws and the tiny brass bowls were empty.

"A camel always knows his way, once he has been over a piece of road," said Lao Wang reflectively. "One night I brought a load of coal from the mountains near my own village of Giao Chung. I was riding this same camel that brought you last night, little Yo Han. The camel had been over the road three weeks before, and it was a full moon, so I slept a little as I rode. When I awoke from my nap, I found my camel balancing on a single wooden beam halfway across the Fen River. The bridge had been swept away by a flood.

"Imagine my fright! There was no way to turn back; nothing to do but go on. My camel set one foot just in front of the other, until we were across. The other twenty followed. Each one knew that a bridge had been there. So each one behaved as though a bridge were still there. It is very strange," he added, "that a beast who can do a thing like that should squeal and stampede when it meets a donkey on a fine, wide piece of road."

While the men slept, John squatted in the innyard as the Chinese children do. He felt like a lizard basking in the March sunshine. The mother camel was standing up so that her baby could suckle. The baby ate noisily, twitching its tale back and forth. When it had drunk its fill, the baby camel wandered out into the sunshine and bumped squarely into a feeding trough.

Then John realized that the little animal could not see. So this was the reason Lao Wang carried the little camel on its mother's back after it was strong enough to walk. He had not noticed before that it was nearly blind, its eyelids caked with yellow matter.

Poor little thing! John put his arms around its velvety neck and stroked its little head. A rope lay at hand with which to make a small halter. John led the baby camel around the yard, between the great kneeling beasts with their heavy tattered fur. In the spring, camels lose their winter coats in great untidy hunks of wool. Many of the animals were half naked, and looked like old beggars with the padding dropping out of their quilted coats.

A bad-tempered camel sneezed at John; the smell was awful, and he hurriedly pulled the baby camel back to its mother. Suddenly over the many noises of the highway outside, he heard a familiar honk—his father's motorcycle already! The "chug-chug" of the engine grew louder and louder and then stopped.

John was at the gate, pulling it open, and in a moment his

father's arms were around him, in a great bear hug. All the village seemed to have followed his father into the courtyard of the Camel Inn. Hundreds of shining black eyes and friendly, curious faces were turned toward them.

"And now, where is the man who sent me the message and took such good care of you?" his father asked. John took him into the inn, where Lao Wang was just rubbing the sleep from his eyes.

"Are you well? Have you eaten?" John's father asked. In Chinese, this is one way to say "good morning."

"Yes, I have eaten, and have you eaten?" Lao Wang replied politely.

"Tell me how you found my son. I have men out looking for him, for miles around Taiku city."

When all the story was told, John's father smiled and said that John must indeed have a terrible desire for travel, to set off for the plains of Mongolia without even a note left behind for his parents.

"But, Father," urged John, "I really do want to go to Mongolia."

"I have been thinking about that trip for our summer vacation, one of these days, John. How would you like to go in the Buick, right over the prairie? It is faster than a caravan, and perhaps we might meet Lao Wang's camels on the way." He turned to the old man. "My friend," he said, "what can I do to show you my gratitude for finding this young scamp, and taking such good care of him?"

"Doctor, if ever I am sick or injured, I will come to you. But right now, there is one small matter. I have a young camel, well-formed and healthy, but it will never be any use to me unless the doctor will take care of its sore eyes. They are so bad that it will certainly become blind."

"Then let us examine the patient," said the doctor. As they got up to go outside, John noticed that the paper windows that let a dim light into the room were pierced with innumerable small holes, such as may be made by pressing a wet finger against paper. At each hole was a shining black eye. As they approached the door, the eyes disappeared. The watchers had taken up another position in order to get the best view of the Americans coming out.

The doctor held the baby camel's head gently as he examined its sore eyes. "This infection can be cured. Bring him to me at the hospital as soon as you can. And now I must be off with this young man. His mother will be impatient to see him. Get up behind me, John. Doughnuts for tea, when we get home."

The motorcycle roared off in a cloud of dust. The curious crowd melted away as quickly as it had gathered, and once more everything was quiet in the courtyard.

A couple of days later the phone rang while John's family were at supper. His mother answered the phone. "A camel to see the doctor," said a voice from the hospital's clinic.

"I don't understand," said John's mother. "Is the name 'Camel'?"

"Oh, no," explained the voice. "A little camel, a blind camel, is waiting to see the doctor."

The doctor hurried through his meal and went directly to the clinic, John trotting eagerly beside him. There was Lao Wang with the great mother camel and the little blind one standing quietly beside her.

The doctor washed the inflamed eyes, and put argyrol in with a medicine dropper. "This treatment must be repeated twice a day for a week or two, and then the little camel will see as well as any other."

"But, Hu Dai Fu, I cannot stay here while my camels eat their bellies full for two whole weeks," objected Lao Wang.

"Let me take care of the little camel," cried John eagerly. "I can teach him to drink cow's milk from a pail just as I did with our calf. I can let him lick milk from my fingers and gradually teach him to drink for himself. And everyday when the other patients come to the clinic, I will lead the little camel over to have his eyes treated."

And so it was arranged. Lao Wang led the mother camel out to join the rest of the caravan, which stood in the shadow of the hospital wall. John watched the string of camels pad majestically down the road. Dust puffed up between their spreading toes, and their great humps and curving necks looked black against the sunset.

The mother camel, with the bell around her neck, was the last in the string. The little camel gave a long "Ma-a-a-a" as he smelled her passing by. "Moo-oo," she replied in her deep voice, and "Cling, clang, clang" her bell sounded through the evening air from far down the road.

—ADELAIDE TRUESDELL

# Wild Geese

The wind blows, the sun shines, the birds sing loud,
The blue, blue sky is flecked with fleecy dappled cloud,
Over earth's rejoicing fields the children dance and sing,
And the frogs pipe in chorus, "It is spring! It is spring!"

The grass comes, the flower laughs where lately lay the snow,
O'er the breezy hill-top hoarsely calls the crow,
By the flowing river the alder catkins swing,
And the sweet song-sparrow cries, "Spring! It is Spring!"

Hark, what a clamor goes winging through the sky!
Look, children! Listen to the sound so wild and high!
Like a peal of broken bells,—kling, klang, kling,—
Far and high the wild geese cry, "Spring! It is spring!"

Bear the winter off with you, O wild geese dear!
Carry all the cold away, far away from here;
Chase the snow into the North, O strong of heart and wing,
While we share the robin's rapture, crying, "Spring! It is spring!"

—CELIA THAXTER

# When Wandering Time Is Come

Glorious it is to see
The caribou flocking down from the forests
And beginning
Their wandering to the north.
Timidly they watch
For the pitfalls of man.
Glorious to see the great herds from the forests
Spreading out over plains of white.
Glorious to see.

Glorious it is to see
Early summer's short-haired caribou
Beginning to wander.
Glorious to see them trot
To and fro
Across the promontories,
Seeking a crossing place.

Glorious it is
To see the long-haired winter caribou
Returning to the forests.
Fearfully they watch
For the little people,
While the herd follows the ebb-mark of the sea
With a storm of clattering hooves.
Glorious it is
When wandering time is come.

—FROM *"Report of the Fifth Thule Expedition"* AND
*Beyond the High Hills* BY KNUD RASMUSSEN

# The Apple Tree

Graceful and lithe and tall,
   It stands by the garden wall,
In the flush of its pink-white bloom
   Elate with its own perfume.
Tossing its young bright head
   In the glad joy of May,
While its singing leaves sing back
   To the bird on the dancing spray,
"I'm alive! I'm abloom!" it cries
   To the winds and the laughing skies.
Ho! for the gay young apple-tree
   That stands by the garden wall!

—LINES FROM *"Poems"*

BY JULIA C. R. DORR

106

# In Time of Silver Rain

In time of silver rain
The earth
Puts forth new life again,
Green grasses grow
And flowers lift their heads,
And over all the plain
The wonder spreads
Of life,
    Of life,
    Of life!

In time of silver rain
The butterflies
Lift silken wings
To catch a rainbow cry,
And trees put forth
New leaves to sing
In joy beneath the sky
As down the roadway
Passing boys and girls
Go singing, too,
In time of silver rain
    When spring
    And life
    Are new.
      —LANGSTON HUGHES

# A Song of Thanks

For the sun that shone at the dawn of spring,
For the flowers which bloom and the birds that sing,
For the verdant robe of the gray old earth,
For her coffers filled with their countless worth,
For the flocks which feed on a thousand hills,
For the rippling streams which turn the mills,
For the lowing herds in the lovely vale,
For the songs of gladness on the gale,—
From the Gulf and the Lakes to the Oceans' banks,—
Lord God of Hosts, we give Thee thanks!

—LINES FROM *"A Song of Thanks"*

BY EDWARD SMYTH JONES

# Joyful Springtime Holidays
## (*Passover and Shavuoth*)

There are three meanings in our great Jewish holidays. Sometimes all three meanings come together on the same day.

First, there are the holidays that celebrate nature. These come in the seasons of planting and of harvest. These are holidays of thanksgiving to the Lord who gave us life and gives life to plants that grow and fish and sheep and deer and birds and all creatures of the earth.

Each time that the crops came up out of the earth, to feed us and to feed all living creatures, our ancestors celebrated the great wonder of life itself. Since they were mostly farmers, they could see this wonder under their own hands, every season.

So we keep the holidays that they made, in the springtime when the earth is ready for seeds. We keep the spring holidays of Passover and Shavuoth. And we keep the holiday of Succoth for the great harvest at the end of summer, when corn is ripe, and when fruit trees are laden with apples, peaches, pears, and other kinds of fruit, and when great bunches of grapes are ripe on the vine. These are the holidays of nature, the holidays of thanks for health and for

the rich joys of living and eating and drinking and feeling the good
things of the world.

Another kind of holiday is the holiday of the spirit. For when
our ancestors felt the joy of life they wanted their lives close to
God. They felt that God gave plenty for all on this earth and that
all people should learn to live in peace according to God's law.

They felt that the laws God gave them, through Moses, were
more wonderful than meat and drink. And these laws kept growing
just as living things keep growing, because in the seed of the Ten
Commandments they saw the whole tree of the laws of society.

These laws are in the Torah. And to celebrate God's giving us
the Torah our ancestors took the same springtime holiday, the joyous
time of Shavuoth, and they said, "What is more joyful to us even
than food and drink?" The answer was "The law! The Torah!" And
so they made Shavuoth the holiday that celebrates the giving of the
Torah. So you can see how there are two reasons for celebrating
Shavuoth.

There is a third kind of holiday that comes from our history. Such holidays celebrate a great event in our history on earth. But they do not celebrate such days only because we had great victories, or because we were saved. Each time, we celebrate a part of our history in which our forefathers saw the work of God.

Passover is such a holiday. As you know, it celebrates a very great event in our history, our escape from slavery in Egypt. But it also has a greater meaning. For it celebrates the idea that God meant each man to be a free person. It celebrates our belief that even if a person makes mistakes, even if people forget the laws of God, they can learn what is right again and win their freedom.

And a great holiday like Passover has the third holiday meaning as well. For Passover comes at the time of an old, old shepherd's festival. When the Jews escaped from Egypt, they remembered the old times, when they were shepherds in their own land. And they remembered their old festivals. Their freedom came at a time of such a festival, and they made this holiday into Passover.

So you see how, on some of our greatest holidays, there are three reasons to celebrate: our very ancient customs in which we thanked God for his beautiful world, our great days in history, and our understanding and love for the life of the spirit.

—MEYER LEVIN AND TOBY K. KURZBAND

# April and May

April cold with dropping rain
Willows and lilacs brings again,
The whistle of returning birds,
And trumpet-lowing of the herds,
The scarlet maple-keys betray
What potent blood hath modest May,
What fiery force the earth renews,
The wealth of forms, the **flush of hues;**
What joy in rosy waves outpoured
Flows from the heart of Love, the Lord.

—FROM *"May-Day"*

BY RALPH WALDO EMERSON

112

# Addir Hu (Glorious He Is)

God of Might, God of Right
   Thee we give all glory,
Thine all praise in these days
   As in ages hoary,
   As in ages hoary.
When we hear, year by year,
   Freedom's wondrous story.

Now as erst, when Thou first
   Mad'st the proclamation
Warning loud, ev'ry proud,
   Ev'ry tyrant nation,
We Thy fame, still proclaim,
   Bow'd in adoration.

Be with all, who in thrall
   To their tasks are driven,
By Thy Power, speed the hour
   When their chains are riven;
Earth around will resound
   Joyful hymns to Heaven.

—TRADITIONAL HEBREW HYMN,
OFTEN SUNG DURING PASSOVER

# Habibi and Yow
## Go to Grandfather's for Seder

"So many people!" exclaimed Habibi, counting the silver wine cups on Grandmother's Seder table. "It looks as though all our aunts and uncles and cousins are coming to the Seder.

Habibi and his little spaniel, Yow, had come to Grandmother and Grandfather for the first Seder. Tomorrow night they would go for Seder to the other Grandmother and Grandfather.

"What would we do if there were three Seders?" Habibi had asked. "We only have two grandmothers and two grandfathers."

Grandmother's table was already set with wine cups and Haggadahs and a beautiful olivewood *matzah* holder for the three whole *matzot* that Grandfather would use for the Seder service.

Yow, Habibi's little black spaniel, was frisking about the room, excited and eager for the relatives to arrive. He liked holiday gatherings, for at these gatherings he was allowed to sit with the guests at the table and to show off some of the tricks Habibi had taught him.

"We're going to have a special guest," Grandmother said. "His name is Eliyahu, Elijah, the Prophet."

"Elijah the Prophet?" Habibi gasped. "Is he coming here tonight, Grandmother? I always wanted to see Elijah the Prophet. Uncle Peter told me that, with four strokes of his wings, Elijah can travel all over the world. He can be everywhere at the same moment. And he doesn't always dress the same or look the same. Sometimes he looks like an old man, sometimes like a beggar, and sometimes he may even be dressed as a prince."

"That's right," said Grandmother, "but the thing to remember is, that wherever Elijah goes, he makes people happy." Grandmother put the largest silver wine cup next to the olivewood *matzah* holder at Grandfather's place.

"For a special guest like Elijah, we must have a special wine cup," she said.

"Elijah, Elijah the Prophet," marveled Habibi, his eyes gazing rapturously upon Elijah's special silver wine cup.

Into the dining room came Mother carrying a large Seder dish. On the Seder dish were grated horseradish and fresh green sprigs of parsley and a roasted shankbone and a roasted egg.

"All we need now is *haroset*," said Grandmother, and she went into the kitchen to mix some fresh *haroset*.

"I'd like to help you, Grandmother," said Habibi stirring the reddish-brown mixture in the bowl. Grandmother added a dash of this and a dash of that.

> "Chopped apples and nuts and sweet, red wine,
> I put in a bowl to mix, mix.
> I then add some cinnamon,—and guess what I have?
> *Haroset*—the color of deep red bricks."

She gave Habibi a teaspoonful to taste. It was sweet and delicious.

One by one the aunts, uncles, and cousins began to arrive, and soon it was time for the Seder to begin. The table stretched from one end of the room to the other and was set with Grandmother's beautiful blue and gold Pesach dishes which she used only during the week of Pesach. The candles gleamed, and the spring flowers in the center of the table were pink and golden and purple. Habibi's cheeks were flushed and Yow's eyes twinkled as he sat perched high on a stool right next to Grandfather. At the head of the table sat Grandfather, dressed in a white robe which he called a *kittel*. On his snow-white head was a white skullcap, at his left, a fluffy white pillow. Father helped pour the Pesach wine into the silver wine cups.

"We'll give a full cup of wine to Elijah," he said, filling Elijah's cup to the very brim.

"Will he drink it all?" asked Habibi, wide-eyed with wonder.

"He may just take one sip," said Father. "After all, he must drink Pesach wine at each Seder all over the world, and a full cup of wine at every Seder might be too much, even for Elijah."

Grandfather raised the first cup of wine. They all rose for *Kiddush*, even Yow. After Kiddush came the moment for which Habibi waited! Grandfather took part of the middle *matzah* from the middle compartment of the olivewood *matzah* holder and hid it carefully under the fluffy white pillow at his left.

"The afikomen!" exclaimed Habibi.

"Yes, the afikomen," said Grandfather, a twinkle in his eye. "And I intend watching it all evening, so don't anyone get a notion to try and take it."

Habibi winked at Uncle Peter. Uncle Peter winked back in a wise, understanding way. They had arranged to work together to secure that piece of *matzah* from under the fluffy white pillow, and

Habibi knew, that with Uncle Peter's help, the afikomen would surely be his. He had already decided on the reward he would ask for its return.

Ruth, Habibi's cousin, opened the front door wide.

"All who are hungry, come in and eat," Grandfather read from the Haggadah. "All who are in need, come in and celebrate the Seder with us."

"Now for *mah nishtanah,* the Four Questions," said Grandfather when the door was closed. "Who will say the *mah nishtanah?*"

All eyes turned to Habibi. He was the youngest at the table.

"I will say the *mah nishtanah,*" said Habibi, and without another word he rose and chanted the *mah nishtanah.* He knew the Four Questions by heart.

"*Mah nishtanah ha-lailah ha-zek mi-kol ha-laylot?*" Why is this night different from all other nights? Why must we eat only *matzah?* Why must we eat bitter herbs? Why must we dip parsley in salt water and bitter herbs in *haroset?* Why must we lean as we sit at the table?"

Grandfather answered Habibi's Four Questions:

"Our forefathers were slaves to Pharaoh in Egypt," he explained. "Tonight we celebrate their freedom from bondage. They had to leave Egypt in great haste and therefore had no time to bake bread, so they took their dough with them and the hot sun baked the dough into flat cakes which they called *matzos.* That is the answer to your first question.

"And now for the answer to your second question. We eat bitter herbs because the Egyptians made the lives of our forefathers very bitter. When we eat the bitter herbs—the horseradish—our eyes fill with tears to remind us of the tears they shed when they were forced by cruel masters to make bricks.

"We dip the parsley in the salt water to show that in the spring-time, green things begin to sprout from the earth, and we dip the bitter herbs into the sweet brick-colored *haroset* to show that even though life was bitter for our forefathers when they made bricks in Egypt, the hope of freedom was sweet. That, Habibi, answers your third question.

"And now for your fourth question. We lean at the table tonight because our forefathers became free men, and free men, in olden times, reclined when they ate."

When the first part of the Seder service was over, a delicious Pesach dinner was served. There were hard-boiled eggs and gefilte fish and knaidel and roast lamb and chicken and tzimmes and so many other good things to eat that Habibi felt as stuffed as a goose. Yow ate and ate so much that he had to get down from his stool and stroll through the rooms for exercise.

At last Habibi saw his chance! Grandfather was telling a story. Father and all the aunts and uncles and cousins were listening to grandfather and had quite forgotten the afikomen. Now his time had come!

Quietly, without a sound, Habibi edged down from his chair and crept softly, slowly, toward the head of the table, toward the place where the fluffy white pillow lay at Grandfather's chair. He slipped his hand underneath, cautiously, stealthily, farther and farther. He felt with his fingers. He felt with his hand. He reached upward and downward, to the right and to the left. But there was no *matzah*. There was no afikomen! For a moment his heart seemed to have stopped beating.

"Who could have taken that afikomen?" he wondered.

He hadn't seen anyone go near the fluffy white pillow, and he had watched closely all evening long. As he made his way back to his chair, sad and disappointed, he caught Uncle Peter's gaze. Uncle Peter smiled and winked his eye.

Habibi's face brightened. "Uncle Peter must have taken the afikomen," he thought. "That's all right. He said he would help me get it." The boy began to feel happy again.

After what seemed ages to Habibi, the meal ended. Grandfather was ready to say grace. But first they must all eat portions of the *afikomen*. Grandfather stuck his hand underneath the fluffy white pillow.

"It's gone!" he announced. "The afikomen has been taken."

Habibi's eyes sparkled. He knew who had the afikomen. Soon he would ask for his reward, and Grandfather would have to give it to him, for otherwise he would not return the *afikomen* and then how could Grandfather conclude the Seder? He smiled at Uncle Peter. Uncle Peter smiled back.

"We must have the *afikomen*," said Grandfather. "We can't proceed without the afikomen."

No one said a word.

"Ruth," asked Grandfather, "did you take the *afikomen?*"

"No, Grandfather," replied Ruth. "I didn't take the *afikomen*."

"Aunt Judith," asked Grandfather, "did you take the *afikomen?*"

"No, I didn't take the afikomen," said Aunt Judith.

"Cousin Elaine, did you take the afikomen?" asked Grandfather.

"No, I didn't take the afikomen," said Cousin Elaine.

"Who then took the afikomen? asked Grandfather. "Someone at this table must have taken the afikomen. We've got to get it back, or we can't proceed with the service. Whoever took the afikomen, speak up!"

Everyone looked at Habibi. He flushed to the roots of his curly red hair.

"Habibi has the afikomen!" they said.

Habibi was embarrassed. He really should have gotten ahead of Uncle Peter. He wished he had taken the afikomen himself.

He went over to Uncle Peter and whispered in Uncle Peter's ear. Uncle Peter's face dropped.

"I haven't got the afikomen," he said. "I thought you took it."

"It wasn't there when I tried to get it. I was so sure that you had it, Uncle Peter." The boy's voice quivered. He was very close to tears.

"Well, where is the afikomen?" everyone asked.

No one at the table seemed to have the afikomen, and no one seemed to know what had become of it.

"This is a nice fix," Grandfather said. "We can't say grace without first eating the afikomen, and we can't open the door for Elijah the Prophet until after we have said grace."

No one knew just what to do. They searched around the chair and under the chair. Perhaps the afikomen had slid down from under the fluffy white pillow. But the afikomen was nowhere in sight. Habibi gazed at the cup of Elijah filled to the brim with Pesach wine.

"How can we keep Elijah the Prophet waiting?" he thought bitterly. "Oh, how can we keep him waiting?" He minded that even more than the reward which he now would not receive.

"I guess we'll have to sit here until morning," said Grandfather.

Everyone was puzzled. No one knew what to do. They had given up all hope of finding the afikomen when suddenly, out of the kitchen, came the little black spaniel with a half cake of *matzah* in his little black mouth.

"YOW! ! !" they all cried together. "Yow, was it you who took the afikomen?"

A smile seemed to flit across Yow's face. He walked directly over to Grandfather with the half cake of *matzah*. Everyone was relieved. Everyone was amused. Yow, the little black dog, had poked his nose under the fluffy white pillow and taken the afikomen. A shout of laughter went up from all at the table. Whoever heard of a dog taking the afikomen? Even Habibi forgot his disappointment and laughed and laughed until the tears rolled down his cheeks.

"That dog," he said. "That little dog! What will he do next?"

"Who will get the reward?" Grandfather asked.

"Why, the dog, of course," everyone replied in unison.

"What can we give a dog?" Grandfather asked.

"I saw the nicest brass collar," Habibi said. "Won't you get that collar for Yow, Grandfather, please?"

Suddenly, from the street, came the sound of dogs barking. It seemed as if all the dogs in the neighborhood were barking together in one voice. Yow heard, and ran to the door.

"Elijah!" said Mother. "When Elijah the Prophet walks through the streets, even the dogs are happy. They bark for joy."

It was then that the door was opened for Elijah the Prophet. Though Habibi strained his eyes and stared with all his might, he he did not see Elijah enter. Cousin Ruth and Aunt Judith insisted they saw him sip some wine from his special wine cup, but Habibi, admitting that the cup did not seem as full of wine as before, was disappointed that he did not get even one glimpse of Elijah.

"It's because you didn't watch closely enough," Uncle Peter said. "Elijah must appear at every Seder in the world tonight, and so he goes out so swiftly, that if you wink an eyelash, you're apt to lose sight of him."

"*Addir Hu, Addir Hu,*" sang Grandfather and all the aunts and uncles and cousins.

Habibi's eyes were beginning to get heavy. Before the *Had Gadya* was finished he was fast asleep.

Mother took him in her arms and carried him to bed.

"No night prayer tonight," she whispered. "On the night when Elijah the Prophet is about, we do not need to say our night prayer. He takes care of all of us."

"Elijah the Prophet," Habibi mumbled, "Elijah the Prophet. To-morrow night at the second Seder, I won't—even—wink an eyelash. Then I'll be sure to see him, won't I, Mother?"

Mother kissed him and turned out the light. Soon Habibi was fast asleep.

And Habibi dreamed that at the second Seder, Elijah came and took the afikomen.

—FROM *Habibi and Yow: A Little Boy and His Dog*

BY ALTHEA O. SILVERMAN

# Play for Shavuoth

It was spring. People went about their work, longing for the war to be over. Mama noticed the shadows deepening on Ella's face because the young man whom she hoped to marry was on active duty. "Ella, there's nothing like work to help you forget trouble." And Ella resolved to heed Mama's advice. She loved dramatics, so she threw herself wholeheartedly into directing plays at Sunday school. For every important Jewish holiday she had the children present a play. Now she was rehearsing the biblical story of Ruth and Naomi for Shavuoth, the Feast of Weeks.

Shavuoth, which comes seven weeks after Passover, commemorates a festival that was held in Palestine in ancient times when the Jews were farmers. At this season of the year, they had finished gathering in their crops. Rejoicing in the harvest, they celebrated by making a pilgrimage to Jerusalem. Each one brought to the Temple the firstfruits of his crop, wheat or barley, dates or figs, olive oil, grapes, and pomegranates. This was to remind them that everything on the earth belongs to the Lord and that man is but the caretaker.

At Shavouth, those who had rich fields were expected to share with the poor and the stranger. The needy were allowed to follow after the gleaners so that they might pick up the fallen grain, or cut the grain in a corner of the field that was set aside especially for them.

But even more important—Shavuoth is the birthday of the Jewish religion. It was at this time that Moses received the Ten Commandments from God on Mount Sinai to give to the people.

One Sunday the children came home from Sunday school, fluttering with excitement. "Mama," Gertie cried, "guess what! You know the play we're rehearsing with Ella? Well—we're going to charge admission and give the money to the Red Cross!"

"That's very good," Mama said. "Whose idea was that?"

"Henny's!" Sarah told her.

"I asked permission from the principal," Henny said proudly, "and he said yes."

"But now that it's all settled," Ella chimed in, "I'm scared to death. Suppose it doesn't turn out well?"

Mama smiled. "It will."

The next three weeks were crowded with preparations for the big event. Ella's guiding hand was in everything. Other teachers did the sewing, but it was Ella who designed the costumes. The scenery was being put together by the older boys, under Ella's watchful eye, and with Ella doing much of the painting. It was Henny who worked out the dances, but it was Ella who offered suggestions. Sometimes she came home in high spirits. Everything was going along fine. Sometimes she despaired of everything. "Mama," she complained, "that girl who's playing Ruth—she's a good actress, and she certainly looks beautiful on the stage, but she'll never be able to sing Ruth's song. I'm going crazy trying to teach her, but it's just no use. She just hasn't got the voice for it."

"Don't take it so to heart," Papa consoled her. "I'm sure no one expects her to be an opera singer. Besides, it's a friendly audience, just the parents and relatives and neighbors. Ten years from now, who'll remember who sang?"

Henny clapped her hands. Her eyes sparkled. "That's it!" she shouted. Rushing over to Ella, she whispered excitedly into her ear. Ella's face lit up.

"What is it? What is it?" the sisters clamored. But neither Henny nor Ella would tell.

Then Shavouth was here. Friends and relatives brought gifts of plants and fruit and shared in the eating of the customary dairy foods that were served for this holiday.

On the Sunday afternoon of the performance, the Hebrew School auditorium was packed. The Healys had been invited to see the play they had heard so much about. They sat in the same row with Papa, Mama, Charlie, Lena, Uncle Hyman, and Mrs. Shiner.

Backstage it was bedlam. Ella and Henny rushed about pinning squirming youngsters into their costumes, putting makeup on their faces, giving last-minute instructions, and in between, hissing, "Shush! They'll hear you outside!"

At the very final moment, Ella yanked away from the curtain a small boy who was peeping out and waving to his mama and papa.

The curtain went up. A spotlight revealed a little girl standing at one side of the stage. She began to read:

"And it came to pass that there was a famine in the land of Judah. And a certain man of Bethlehem went to live in the fields of Moab, he and his wife, and his two sons. And the man was named Elimelich and his wife was named Naomi. . . .

Elimelich died. And the two sons took wives of the women of Moab—the name of the one was Orpah and the name of the other

Ruth, and they dwelt there about ten years. And the sons died and the three women were left widowed. Naomi wished to return to the land of her fathers, and Ruth and Orpah went with her through the fields to the road that led to Bethlehem."

"Isn't that from the Bible?" Mrs. Healy whispered to Papa.

"Well, it's not exactly like we read it in the synagogue. I suppose they made it simple so the children would understand."

The reader closed her book and disappeared. The stage lights brightened.

"See, Charlie," Mama said softly, "that's Ruth, and that's Orpah, and there is Naomi."

Charlie scoffed. "Nah! That's not Naomi. That's Sarah. She's dressed up like an old lady."

Naomi stretched out her arms and began to speak in a broken voice. "Alas, soon it will be dark. Return you now to your homes."

And Orpah, weeping bitterly, embraced Naomi and departed.

Then Naomi said to Ruth, "Dearest Ruth, go you too as Orpah has done. I am an old woman, but you are still young. Your husband is dead, but here in the land of Moab you have many relatives and friends. You will find happiness with them again."

But no matter how much Naomi urged, Ruth would not leave. Lifting her head she began to sing. The audience grew still under the spell of the lovely voice, so full and strong, yet so tender.

Papa and Mama exchanged bewildered glances. The voice— they knew it so well! But how could it be? There was the girl on the stage singing the role of Ruth. Her mouth moved in song. Her whole body seemed alive with the music. They listened intently "It *is* Ella singing!" Mama whispered.

"No mistake about it," Papa whispered back.

They marveled how cleverly it was being done. Ruth's lips moved perfectly in time with Ella's backstage singing. Pure and clear were the beautiful words of devotion that have come down through the ages:

> Entreat me not to leave thee
> And to return from following after thee
> For whither thou goest, I will go
> And where thou lodgest, I will lodge
> Thy people shall be my people
> And thy God my God.
>
> Where thou diest, will I die
> And there will I be buried.
> The Lord do so to me and more also
> If aught but death part thee and me.

The curtain was lowered, and the applause rang out. Murmurs of admiration swelled from all sides of the auditorium. "Such a wonderful voice!"

Mama and Papa smiled at each other.

Grace leaned over and touched Mama's hand. "You know, I would have sworn that was Ella singing."

Mama's eyes twinkled. "You think so?"

Act Two began almost immediately. Once again the reader stood in a circle of light.

"Now it happened that Ruth and Naomi came to Bethlehem at the time of the harvest. There was a man called Boaz, kinsman to Naomi, and he had many large fields. And Ruth joined the poor who followed after the gleaners in the fields of Boaz, for it was known that he was kind and generous."

Bright light flooded the stage, and signs of delight rippled through the audience, so charming was the picture. The golden fields filled with cut sheaves seemed so real that one could almost smell the fallen gleanings. Slowly the gleaners moved across the stage gathering up the grain. Ruth was among them, and the others gazed at her and whispered about her great beauty.

Boaz appeared. "Who is this maiden?" he asked of his gleaners.

"She is the daughter-in-law of thy kinswoman, Naomi. They have just come from the land of Moab."

"Ah, yes, so I have heard. They have suffered much and are in great need. See that you let many stalks fall in the maiden's path."

Then Boaz addressed himself to Ruth. "I bid you welcome. Come to my fields as often as you like for the grain with which to make your bread. You shall eat with my workers when you are hungry, and if you are thirsty, they will draw water for you to drink."

"Why are you so kind to me?" Ruth asked.

And Boaz replied, "It has been told to me all that you have done for Naomi. Who deserves kindness more than you who have been so loyal and generous to an old woman?"

Soon the harvest gatherers laid aside their scythes and sat down to eat and drink and make merry. "Come, let us dance!" cried one, and in a moment a small group leaped to their feet. Among the dancers were Gertie and Charlotte.

The piano gave forth a rollicking tune, and the gleaners burst into song, clapping their hands in rhythm. Skirts billowing gracefully, heads proudly raised, the little dancers circled about. "Did you ever see a prettier sight!" exclaimed Mrs. Healy.

Caught up in the happy beat of the music, the audience began clapping their hands and stamping their feet. Backstage, Ella and Henny hugged each other. "They like it! They really like it!"

Hopping and skipping for all she was worth, Gertie was leading the line of dancers when suddenly she heard—snap! The safety pin holding her skirt band flew open! She could feel the skirt beginning to slip down the back. Desperately she clung to it with one hand, trying to face front all the time. Already some people in the front row were tittering. Oh, dear, what should she do? She turned her head toward the wings, sending appealing glances for help.

Frantically, Ella beckoned to her. Gertie started to dance sideways, forcing herself to smile. But before she could reach the wings, the droopy skirt was trailing on the floor. The titters grew into boisterous laughter. Gertie ran sobbing off the stage.

Ella caught her. "It's all right, Gertie. They're not laughing at you. They're laughing with you!" Quickly she pinned the unruly skirt back into place. "Go on back!" and she gave her a little push.

Sniffing a little, Gertie skipped back to her place among the dancers. The audience applauded loudly.

"They're clapping for you," Charlotte murmured to Gertie as she danced by.

"Honest?" Gertie asked, and her eyes glowed.

Without further mishap, the play went into Act Three. Boaz, the rich landowner, grew to love Ruth; they were married and lived happily ever after. Thus the play ended. Everyone agreed that it had been a huge success.

That night the family sat around the table eating the traditional blintzes, the pancakes filled with sweetened cheese that everyone loved. The talk was of nothing but the play. "Just think," Ella said, "besides all the fun we had, we made one hundred and twenty-five dollars for the Red Cross!"

"Ella, I thought you said the girl who played Ruth couldn't sing a note," Papa remarked, merry crinkles showing around his eyes.

Laughter rolled around the table. "Wasn't it amazing the way it was done?" Sarah said, enthusiastically. "The audience never even guessed."

"It was Henny's idea," Ella put in. "You were really smart, Henny."

"Nope. Not at all," replied Henny. "Actually it was Papa who gave me the idea."

Papa looked puzzled. "Who? Me?"

"Don't you remember, Papa? You said, 'Ten years from now, who'll remember who sang?' That's when it came to me like a flash!"

"Well, so I'm the smart one!" Papa exclaimed, looking pleased at everyone.

—SYDNEY TAYLOR

# Daffodils

In spite of cold and chills
 That usher in the early spring,
We have the daffodils.
 —TRANSLATION BY W. N. PORTER

# Spring Festivals
## (*Passover and Shabuoth*)

The last few days before Passover always seemed to Miriam the busiest days of the whole year. There was a visit to the dressmaker to fetch home the new dress she had been thinking about for weeks, for what is Passover without new clothes? Then little David had to be taken downtown for new shoes.

David was also busy, running to the Jewish grocery store for mother, to bring home horseradish and more eggs and big square boxes of *matzos*. And not only the family but the house had to be made ready to greet the Passover in a clean, fresh spring dress. Floors were scrubbed and clean curtains hung and rugs cleaned; the Passover dishes, used only for this one week in the whole year, were washed, and the Passover silver was polished until it shone.

For once father had to help with the housework. According to old custom it is the duty of the man of the family to search for leaven after the house has been made ready for the Passover, or Pesach.

Passover is one of the three great pilgrim feasts of Jewish people. It marks the passing of winter into spring, and no doubt it began as a nature feast; the name, Pesach, comes from a Hebrew word meaning skip, or dance, and is thought to refer to the skipping of the young lambs. So in earliest times this was very likely a feast the shepherds kept before starting out to look for new pastures for their flocks. Later, when the wandering shepherds became farmers and settled in Palestine, offerings were taken to the Temple at Jerusalem. In the Book of Leviticus, the Israelites were commanded to bring as their offerings a lamb one year old without any blemish and a sheaf of grain from the first harvest, which falls earlier in the warm climate of Palestine than in this country.

But the historical beginnings of the Feast of the Passover are much more important. Passover falls on the fifteenth day of the first month of the Jewish calendar; Nisan was made the first month because it is the birth month of Israel as a nation. It marks the beginning of the history of the Jews as a free people, for the name Passover suggests how they, escaping from their Egyptian slavery, passed through the Red Sea, "from darkness into light, from slavery into freedom." The name also refers to the story of the Angel of Death, who slew the firstborn of Egypt, but passed over the firstborn of the Israelites, whose houses were marked with the blood of the newly sacrificed paschal lamb.

The story of the Deliverance from Egypt tells how Moses, after pleading in vain with Pharaoh to allow the children of Israel to go free, bade them sacrifice the paschal lamb and make ready for their long journey into the desert. We are told that in their haste to leave the land of bondage where they had known such cruel hardships the Israelites set out with dough still in their kneading troughs; this was later baked in the hot desert sun, forming thin flat cakes, much like the matzos eaten during the Passover season. In memory of the flight from Egypt and the birth of Israel as a free nation, the descendants of these desert wanderers were commanded to keep the

Feast of the Unleavened Bread. Even to our day matzos are eaten
for a whole week, which, when the festival is strictly observed, is
ushered in by the Search after Leaven.

It is leaven in bread and other foods which causes fermenta-
tion. None of this is to be allowed in the house during the eight days
of Passover. So yesterday father passed from room to room in search
of Hometz (leaven). When the last crumb was gathered he thanked
God, praying also that any bit which may have been overlooked
be "destroyed and be like the dust of the earth."

But now it is time for the Seder! Seder really means order (of
the feast) or service; to Jewish children it has always meant the
most wonderful Jewish holiday meal of the whole year. As soon as
father returns from synagogue he takes his place at the head of

the table; tonight his chair is heaped high with cushions to represent the couches once used at the festive meal. In olden days only free men were allowed to recline at meals while slaves stood and served them. On this night of freedom the Jews, no matter how enslaved and ground down they were by their enemies, rested on cushions like free men, in remembrance of the freedom which had come to them on the first Passover.

Beside father's place is an empty chair for Elijah, who is expected to visit every Seder table; for it is Elijah the Friend who will usher in the Messiah to free Israel. So what better time to expect him than on Israel's Night of Freedom? The large goblet of wine on the table is also reserved for Elijah.

The larger platter before father bears the various symbols of the feast. First, the folded napkin with three matzos placed one between each fold, each piece of unleavened bread representing a division of the Jewish people, Cohen, Levi, and Israelite. The lamb bone represents the sacrificial lamb; the roasted egg is a symbol of hope and resurrection; from the seemingly dead egg comes life, from winter spring, from slavery freedom. The parsley and the horseradish root are the greens typifying spring; later the parsley is dipped into salt water (tears shed in slavery) and the bitter horseradish root eaten with *Haroset* (a mixture of apples and nuts and wine) which by its red color suggests the bricks made during Egyptian slavery. Life holds both bitter and sweet, as Jews must have remembered at their Passover feasts year after year, often in lands where they were hated and hunted and put to death for their religion. Yet they never lost courage, and every Passover festival ended with the old hope: We celebrate Passover this year in the land of exile; but next year we will spend it in Jerusalem.

One of the most important parts of the Seder is the Four Quotations asked by the youngest child, who inquired concerning the meaning of the feast. Little Joseph was very proud of being allowed to ask them this year; his uncle answered him and explained the meaning of the symbols on the Seder dish. Another feature of the service, which is meant to keep the children interested during the long evening of prayers and explanations, is the hiding of the matzos. Part of the middle matzah is kept for the afikomen (dessert); part is hidden and the child finding it may expect a present.

But perhaps the children like best Chad Gadyah, the story written in Aramaic and sung to an old melody, which tells of the Kid (Israel) that my Father (God) bought for two pieces of money (the two tablets on which the Ten Commandments were written). It is one of the world's oldest nursery rhymes, like the House that Jack Built. But it has deep religious meaning, and every figure in it represents a great event in the long, wonderful history of the Jewish people.

A child is usually asked to open the door during the service, to invite the stranger who may be passing to come in. This custom may go back to the days when the Jews were accused of using human blood at their festival and wanted to show that they had nothing to conceal from their neighbors.

Like Succoth, the autumn festival, the first two and last two days of the Passover festival are observed. The Song of Songs is read during the synagogue service; as a story of spring in Palestine it is appropriate for a springtide holyday. Because it tells the love story of a beautiful shepherdess and contains several marriage songs, it also reminds us of God's love for Israel whom he led out of Egypt.

After the service on the eve of the second day of Passover the counting of the omer begins. An omer (which here is used to mean harvest) is a measure about the size of a half-gallon; it contains some of the wheat of the first harvest, which was brought as an offering for the priests at Jerusalem. This counting lasts for seven weeks. The days of counting are called Sephirah days. Neither marriages nor feasts may take place during Sephirah days, with the exception of the New Moon and the thirty-third day of the omer, which is known as Lag B'omer.

Lag B'omer, also known as the Scholar's Holiday, is a time of rejoicing; for on that day, we are told, the prayers of the pupils of the gentle sage, Rabbi Akiba, brought about the end of a terrible plague in Palestine. Miriam's Hebrew School gave a Lag B'omer party. There were refreshments and a play about Rabbi Akiba and Bar Kochba, the last of the Jewish warriors against the ancient Roman Empire. Afterwards the children had an archery contest. Since Miriam had been given a bow and arrows for finding the afikomen at the Seder, she had been practicing ever since, and now won the archery prize.

After the fifty days, or seven weeks, of counting the omer comes Shabuoth, the Feast of Weeks. Shabuoth is chiefly a festival of the synagogue where special services are held for two days. In the home it is sometimes celebrated by serving dairy foods, as milk is especially plentiful in Palestine that season of the year. Honey is also eaten to remind us of the sweetness of the Torah, the wonderful Law which God gave to Moses that day.

"Shabuoth," as father explained to the children, "is one of the great pilgrim feasts like Passover and Succoth. It is sometimes called the Festival of the Firstfruits, because after the counting of the omer an offering of firstfruits was brought to the Temple at Jerusalem. This offering was arranged in a special way, with barley at the bottom of the basket and wheat above; over the wheat they placed olives, then dates, and finally figs; this was beautifully decorated with leaves. Another offering was the twin loaves made out of the new grain. Later when there was no Temple to which to bring offerings, the Jews decorated their synagogues with flowers and spread fresh grass upon the floor to celebrate the giving of the Law."

"Then Shabuoth is another farmer, or nature, holiday," said Miriam.

"Yes. But the historical part is most important. Most people believe that Shabuoth is the greatest day in the national history of Israel. On Passover the people became a free nation, but on Shabuoth they received the Ten Commandments. Now instead of being a little desert tribe they became the nation that was to influence all mankind. For all civilized men today base their laws on their commandments which the Children of Israel received as they stood at the foot of Mount Sinai.

"You know the story of Ruth, children," continued Father. "How she was a stranger from the land of Moab and came to Israel with her dead husband's mother, Naomi. She was not only a good daughter to Naomi; she accepted the religion of Israel and obeyed faithfully. Because Ruth was so loyal to the Law, her story in the Book of Ruth is read in the synagogue services at Shabuoth. There is also a legend that King David was born and died on Shabuoth; so it is appropriate to read Ruth's story at this spring festival as she was given the honor of becoming the ancestress of this most loved of Jewish kings."

—FROM *With the Jewish Child in Home and Synagogue* BY ELMA EHRLICH LEVINGER

# Spring Music

Oh the brown leaves
Fall in the bitter blast like tears
From an aged widow. . . .
And whispering winds
Steal the violets' breath
And bury their leaves in snow. . . .
And the tides flow back
Like the ebbing years
Into cool immunity.
But memory's voice,
Like the music of waves,
Sings April tunes
    Forever.

—ARNA BONTEMPS

# April Rain Song

Let the rain kiss you.
Let the rain beat upon your head with silver liquid drops.
Let the rain sing you a lullaby.
The rain makes still pools on the sidewalk.
The rain makes running pools in the gutter.
The rain plays a little sleep-song on our roof at night—
And I love the rain.

—LANGSTON HUGHES

# Go, Ploughman, Plough

Go, ploughman, plough
The mearing lands,
The meadow lands,
The mountain lands:
All life is bare
Beneath your share,
All love is in your lusty hands.

Up, horses, now!
And straight and true
Let every broken furrow run:
The strength you sweat
Shall blossom yet
In golden glory to the sun.

—JOSEPH CAMPBELL

# Australian Spring

Lightly the breath of the spring wind blows,
   Though laden with faint perfume;
'Tis the fragrance rare that the bushman knows,
   The scent of the wattle bloom.
Two-thirds of our journey at least are done,
   Old horse! Let us take a spell
In the shade from the glare of the noonday sun,
   Thus far we have travelled well;
Your bridle I'll slip, your saddle ungirth,
   And lay them beside this log,
For you'll roll in that track of reddish earth,
   And shake like a water-dog.

              —ADAM LINDSAY GORDON

# Earth's Youngest Daughter

What shall she have,
   Earth's youngest daughter?
Green combs of willow wands,
   Mirrors in the water.

Where shall we go
   To do her birthday honour?
Clematis above the rocks
   Hangs her silken banner.

Heath lights tapers through the bush—
   White, and red for morning;
All the tight-balled wattle boughs
   Overnight are turning

Each into a golden fleece,
   Rich as Jason plundered,
Where across the shining weir
   Winter floods had thundered.

Reedy singers call her home,
   Little Proserpine,
Cuckoo's flute, dark bittern's drum,
   And wren pipes fine.

Old as moss in glacier lands—
   Earth's youngest daughter—
Clean as worship in the hills—
   New as lambs and laughter.

              —M. FINNIN

# The Bush

But we have heard the bell-birds ring
Their silver bells at eventide,
Like fairies on the mountain side—
The sweetest note man ever heard.

The wild thrush lifts a note of mirth;
The bronzewing pigeons call and coo
Beside their nests the long day through;
The magpie warbles clear and strong
A joyous glad, thanksgiving song,
For all God's mercies upon earth.

And many voices such as these
Are joyful sounds for those to tell,
Who know the bush and love it well,
With all its hidden mysteries.

For us the roving breezes bring
From many a blossom-tufted tree—
Where wild bees murmur dreamily—
The honey-laden breath of spring.
—LINES FROM *"Song of the Future"*
BY A. B. PATERSON

# Preparing for Easter
## (*The Lenten Season*)

Lent, the forty days before Easter, is a period when many Christians prepare their lives and hearts for Eastertide. Lent, the Anglo-Saxon word for spring, means "the season of lengthening days."

As winter food ran low, before the sun was warm enough for spring planting, ancient pagans often fasted on certain days. They sacrificed to their gods and repented of anything that would have offended them. Some of the ancient springtime customs have been adopted and changed and made a part of the reverent Christian Lenten and Easter seasons.

Today during Lent some do without luxuries or favorite foods to increase their devotion and permit them to better appreciate the events of Easter. With the money saved, many give food and clothing to the needy throughout the world.

Shrove Tuesday, the day before Lent begins, is devoted to prayer and repentance of wrongs. It is sometimes called Fat Tuesday and Pancake Tuesday. Long before the days of refrigeration, when eggs, butter, and oils had to be used before the Lenten fasting began, the last fried foods until Easter were often rich egg pancakes.

147

Tradition records that when the church bells tolled on Shrove Tuesday in 1445, in Olney, England, a hungry housewife, making pancakes for lunch, carried them on the griddle to church. It was such a funny sight that Olney made pancake-racing a yearly event.

And in 1950 some churchwomen in Liberal, Kansas, raced a quarter of a mile, carrying pancakes on griddles, to start the yearly Pancake Race. Now runners in Olney, England, and in Liberal, Kansas, challenge each other. Runners race the same distance, then compare their times by telephone.

Tasty doughnuts without holes, called Fastnachtskuchen or Fast Night Cakes, are eaten on Shrove Tuesday in Germany and in several other countries, including parts of the United States. Hot cross buns are a Lenten specialty in some areas. In certain places they are eaten during all the forty days of Lent, in others just on the first day, and in still others hot cross buns are eaten the third day before Easter.

On Wednesday, the first day of Lent, some Christians observe the tradition of putting ashes on their foreheads. Many churches unite in a World Day of Prayer on the first Friday in Lent with petitions for peace and goodwill throughout the world.

Remnants of ancient folk customs still exist. On the first Sunday of Lent, called Fire Sunday or Brandsonntag in southern Germany and the Festival of the Torches in France, people run through the streets with firebrands that symbolically chase away winter and bring spring's warmth. Straw figures of Old Man Winter are burned at this season in parts of Switzerland.

Holy Week, the week before Easter, begins with Palm Sunday in remembrance of the day Jesus rode into Jerusalem amid crowds cheering and waving palms. Throughout the Christian world this is a day observed with great reverence.

The following Thursday, the Thursday before Easter, is called Maundy Thursday. No one really knows where the name originated. Some say Maundy is derived from *Mande,* an Old French word whose Latin original meant command or mandate, and that it refers to Jesus' mandate to his followers, "That you love one another." Others say the word is from the Anglo-Saxon *Maund* which means basket. Many years ago in England women went about with alms baskets on that day giving gifts to the poor.

Good Friday, also called Long Friday, Great Friday, or God's Friday, is a day of prayer and meditation. Some Christian churches hold the Service of the Three Hours, others tell the Passion story in music. All is preparation for the glorious celebration of Easter soon to arrive.

—MILDRED  CORELL  LUCKHARDT

# Happy Easter!

" 'Welcome, happy morning!' age to age shall say." This is the beginning of an Easter hymn that has been translated into many languages from a long Easter-springtime festival poem written in Latin in the sixth century by an Italian who became a bishop in France. It is still sung today in many different churches around the world and expresses the joy with which Christians celebrate Easter. The inspiration for this and other Easter hymns springs from the stories of the first Easter. Although these stories first were written in Greek, they, too, have been translated into hundreds of languages and are read joyfully every year by many people in churches and family groups at Eastertime.

Hope and new life are part of the Easter celebration, and the songs of joy have come from many lands and many centuries. In the eighth century when Damascus was the seat of government and religion of the Mohammedan Omaiyads, a young Christian who grew up there wrote joyful Easter songs. John of Damascus, as he became known, gathered Christians together to celebrate Easter with hope and to sing, "The day of resurrection! Earth tell it out abroad."

Although the origin of many Easter songs and customs can be traced back for centuries, nobody is certain just how the name Easter came to be connected with the Christian celebration. Many say that the word "Easter" comes from a springtime festival which a number of ancient nations devoted to the goddess of spring, Eastur or Oestre or some similar name, and celebrated the return of sunshine which brought new life. Some scholars say that the word "Easter," like the German word "Ostern," comes from Norse words such as Ostara, which meant "the season of new birth" or the "season of the growing sun." Since "ost" or "east" is the place where the sun rises, some people think that the name Easter originally was connected with the season of the year and not with a pagan goddess.

In any event, Easter is celebrated at the time of the growing sun and of new birth, the season when many ancient peoples were happy because of the end of winter and the "resurrection of the sun." So it is that many happy springtime customs from many people, times, and places have become part of the Easter festival.

The date of Easter was fixed by the Council of Nicea, called together by the Emperor Constantine in A.D. 325 at Nicea, an ancient town in Asia Minor. The Council had directed astronomers in Egypt who were skilled in calculating dates according to the course of heavenly bodies, to help determine for the Church the date when all Christians might celebrate Easter. As a result, for more than sixteen hundred years Easter has been celebrated by millions of Christians on the first Sunday following the full moon that appears after the spring, or vernal, equinox. Since this equinox, the time when the sun crosses the celestial equator when day and night are equal in length, occurs about March 21, Easter cannot be observed before March 22 or after April 25.

Eastern Orthodox churches who use the Julian calendar and not the Gregorian, generally celebrate Easter on a spring Sunday different from Western churches, with beautiful music, ceremonies, and joyful customs. The Greek word for Passover is Pascha, and many Europeans refer to Easter by that name or words derived from it; for the original Good Friday also was the Jewish Passover.

When Ponce de Leon sighted land in the New World on Easter morning, March 27, 1513, he gave it the name Florida, for Pascua Florida had come to be the Spanish name for all of Holy Week. Naturally, such navigators as he were very aware of the phases of the moon and especially at the time of the spring equinox.

Since the date of Easter follows the appearance of the spring full moon, and since in many lands from ancient times a hare has been connected in people's minds with the moon, hares and rabbits have become pleasant symbols of Easter festival and of new life at springtime. The egg always has been a symbol of new life, also, for although it looks dead it carries life within itself. Far back in history there are accounts of such people as the Egyptians giving eggs to each other, with good wishes for life and growth. And from ancient times, the Hebrews, who remembered their escape from Egyptian slavery at Passover, made the Paschal egg an important part of their festival meal.

The date of the beginning of the custom of coloring Easter eggs is not known for certain, but there is an old record that in 1290 King Edward I of England bought more than thirty-seven dozen eggs to be colored and covered with gold leaf, as gifts to members of the royal household. Ukranians with their pysanki have long made very beautiful colored eggs, and some of them have been kept as heirlooms from generation to generation. Many charming stories are told in a number of countries about colored eggs.

Nobody knows for sure just when Easter eggs and the Easter

rabbit became associated, nor just how the jolly fairy tale about rabbits bringing colored eggs began. Yet a German book in the late seventeenth century refers to the story of the bunny's laying eggs and hiding them in the garden, and speaks of it as a very old fable. It may be that the old folktale of the Easter bunny and eggs began in Germany centuries ago.

Egg hunts are part of Easter fun, and people in many lands have enjoyed many different Easter games. Many people take part in Egg-rolling, including that on the White House lawn in Washington.

Water, also, because it is necessary for life and growth and because it purifies and makes clean, plays a part of the Easter celebration in many lands. Not only does sprinkling with water become sort of an Eastertime game among many children, but it is a springtime custom in several religions.

Singing and dancing long have enlivened the Easter festival. Many people used to say "the sun dances at Easter," and they, too, danced; and often people have gone out at Easter dawn to "watch the sun dance for joy."

All over the world in different settings, Christians gather to watch the Easter sunrise and sing hymns and listen to the Easter story once more. In many places Greek Orthodox Christians gather on Easter Eve for a beautiful ritual, and at midnight, carrying lighted candles, go out into the darkness to look for Jesus. After the search the priest chants joyfully, "The Lord Jesus is risen!" And the people sing out, "He is risen!" and hold their lights high.

Not only is Easter a time of worship and festivity, but most Christians give special Easter offerings through their churches so that the poor and suffering of the world may have new life. And in this springtime of the year when Jews have been celebrating Passover and remembering with kindness the poor and oppressed of the world, numbers of people of goodwill from many different backgrounds join together in raising money to help crippled children. They want these children to have "new life and activity . . . physically, mentally and spiritually."

Celebrating the new life at this time of year, a favorite carol begins:

Spring has unwrapped the flowers, day is fast reviving,
Life in all her growing powers, toward the light is striving.

—MILDRED CORELL LUCKHARDT

# Easter

The air is like a butterfly
   With frail blue wings,
The happy earth looks at the sky
   And sings.

—JOYCE KILMER

# Christophilos
## and the Pascal Lamb

It was the time of the year when fishermen paint their boats. In the little village in Greece where Christophilos lived, some of them could not afford paint, and those who had no money stood along the shore or sat in cafes on the seafront and said it was too early to paint the boats.

The octopuses in the sea and the hens in the village were preparing to lay their spring eggs. Of course an octopus' egg is of importance only to an octopus; but in their way they are just as fussy over them as hens are.

Yaryar, Christophilos' grandmother, said it was not the time of the year to shed one's clothes, although the sun had teeth, and Christophilos' neighbor said that even a donkey knew that and that is why they drop their coats so slowly.

Everything in the world knew it was spring. White herons mated along the shore, and dolphins wheeled in the sea near the tower. The sun drew so much color out of the sky and dropped it into the sea that men paused on their way to work to admire the brilliant, glistening waves.

It was the Easter fast, and everybody ate dry bread and olives and young green garlic and weeds from the fields. Only the babies drank milk. The whole village prepared for Easter. Houses were whitewashed inside and out, and those who could not afford to buy whitewash stole it from their neighbors. Every man kept a careful watch on his lime pit. Yaryar even whitewashed the big cobblestones in the floor, so that it looked very clean indeed.

On calm days boats stole out to fish for octopuses, and when the afternoon breeze came up and spoiled the fishing you could hear the flap, flap, slap, slap of octopuses being beaten along the shore. And you could see a long line of men rubbing and stroking and beating them until they were tender enough for the pot. Octopus is neither fish nor meat and can be eaten all the year round, even in the Easter fast.

Octopus poles on either side of the boats were hung with long, lank octopuses drying in the sun, and by day and night the smell of them hung over the village.

One day the swifts came back to the tower, helter-skelter, from the lands they had wintered in, and there began a great clamor and the rush of wings up and down the chutes outside the top of the tower. The swifts built their nests in the chutes, but the swallows flew into the tower and stuck their nests all over the big, old wooden beams. They passed in and out of the windows and arrow holes as they had done for hundreds and hundreds of years.

The world climbed up and down the stairs twice a day to church; the old people and the young people and the women with babies. They sighed as they climbed because the tower was so high and the stairs so steep, and the old people felt it was such a labor that their hearts must really break; but they all went.

The men of the village walked among their herds each day and poked the baby goats in the ribs to see which was the fattest because every household had to kill a fine fat kid for Easter. The mother of Christophilos had only she-goats, and she thought it terrible to kill a little she-goat for eating.

Yaryar said, "Change the she-goat for a little he-goat, and kill that."

"Who would give away a good she-goat for a he-goat?" asked Christophilos' mother. "Only a fool would do that. I will kill Mavroula, the wild pig."

This shocked everyone very much indeed, because the world knew that Mavroula, the wild pig, had been suckled by a dog, and they believed that her flesh had become the same as a dog's. To eat dog's flesh is shameful, but to eat it at Easter would be terrible. The boys called "Dog eater!" after Christophilos, as he walked through the village, and at last he felt that it was more than he could bear. But his mother was a very determined woman, and the more people cried "Dog eater!" the more she intended to kill Mavroula.

Yaryar cried for two whole days, and then said she would pass Easter fasting unless she could eat with the neighbors, for never in her whole life had she done anything so sinful as to eat dog's meat.

Easter is a very joyful occasion, and everyone should eat lambs, because lambs are young and joyful. That has been the custom from very old times indeed.

The lamb must be killed on the threshold of the house at midday, the day before Easter Sunday, and it must be roasted in the great village oven at night while everyone is at the Easter Service. It must be finished when the guns go off, and the people shout to each other, "Christ has risen! Truly He has risen!" And all the children crack colored Easter eggs.

The old tower becomes lively and wonderful at Easter, blazing with candles. Up and down the stairs, and on the landings, and in the big empty rooms. Everyone holds a candle and sometimes two. Big fat brown candles made of beeswax and big fat white candles made of tallow. They take the holy fire from the priest on Easter night, and then carry their candles home through the village in procession, sheltering the lights with their hands. They laugh and drop candle grease over each other, and if a candle blows out, a dozen offer light to it, so that each house has its own portion of holy fire for the year.

Then the lambs are eaten with great rejoicing, even if they are only goats. But how could anyone rejoice over a wild pig that has been suckled by a dog? Christophilos spoke to the priest about it, but the priest was only thinking about Easter, and he said, "Speak to me afterwards, boy," and he got off his chair and limped about his room. Christophilos knew that after Easter would be too late.

When he got home he found his mother angry and red in the face. She stood in the middle of the room talking fast and loud, and Yaryar crouched on her heels spinning wool with a hand spindle.

"I carry more brushwood to the village oven than any other woman, and I've always done so," cried Christophilos' mother as he came in, "and now the women dare say that I cannot roast Mavroula, the wild pig, in the oven! We'll see who's who when the time comes! If necessary I will cook her on a spit over charcoal in the village square!"

"It is unwise to go against the world—" began Yaryar, but Christophilos' mother stamped her foot, and cried, "A!" which is a term of great contempt. Then she turned on Christophilos.

"Are you a little goat, that you play!" she cried. "Go to the forest with the little pig and feed her there!"

"It's going to rain," said Yaryar. "See how low the swallows fly."

"Rain, or no rain the pig must go to the forest," she cried.

Christophilos took Mavroula out of the house. She trotted briskly along beside him on her toe-tips, running on ahead and grunting back at him, nosing everything out of curiosity. He used to be proud of her following him, because everyone used to say, "There goes Christophilos and his wild pig." They nodded their heads and told strangers how he caught her himself when she was very small. Now they all cried "Dog eater!" after him, and he felt terribly ashamed. He found a choice spot for Mavroula and drove the peg of her rope into the ground, and she began to enjoy herself grunting and rooting as all pigs do.

Christophilos thought how good it would be if she broke her rope and ran off and became wild again; but he didn't dare to let her go because of his mother's anger. Then he heard a monk singing along the forest road, and he was singing an old song to keep the devil off his path. He walked very fast, leading a mule loaded with wine, and the wine was in pigskins tied with thongs of leather round the neck and four legs. The legs stuck out fat and funny, and the wine churned in the skins and made them wobble as the mule walked.

"Ho, Christophilos!" cried the monk, and at that moment the mule stepped on a small stone, which slipped under its shoe.

"There!" cried the monk, "that is because I stopped singing for protection against the devil!" He made a funny face at Christophilos and dropped the rope of the mule's halter, which was plastered with blue beads for luck and had a knot of garlic plaited into it against the evil eye.

Christophilos ran to help the monk because he was naturally a helpful boy; and because the monk was old and stout and breathed heavily when he stooped. Christophilos picked up the mule's foot

and held it between his knees. The monk pulled a long, hooked knife out of his pocket under his gown, and between them they got out the stone.

While they worked, Mavroula, who was exceedingly inquisitive, sniffed at the calves of the monk's great legs. The monk was very pleased with Christophilos and very interested in Mavroula, and he wanted to know how Christophilos had caught her. Christophilos told him everything. He even told him how they must eat Mavroula when the dear Christ had risen, and everyone else was joyfully eating lamb.

"But," said the monk, "that is a sin. She has been suckled by a dog. You must let her go to the forest again."

Then he suddenly remembered his grapes, and how the wild pigs came each summer and spoilt the vineyards in spite of a guard of eighty monks with stout sticks and tin cans to beat them off with, and in spite of blazing bonfires and a great deal of fuss and noise.

"No, that won't do at all," he said quickly. "There are too many wild pigs!" Then he saw Christophilos' sad face, and he cried, "I have it! I am going to sell my wine in the town of Errisos, and I have a spare sack to bring things back to the monastery in. I will carry Mavroula off in it, and sell her for you in the market, and I will buy a fat Easter lamb with the money!"

"A lamb!" cried Christophilos, "but that would be wonderful! No one in our village eats lamb, because we have only goats."

So they tied Mavroula in the sack and hung her among the sacks of wine, and she squealed and yelled as the monk hurried her through the village, but Christophilos' mother never guessed it was Mavroula when she saw the monk leading the mule past her house. But when Christophilos went home and told her what had happened, she was very angry indeed, so angry that she took a stick and Christophilos into the yard, meaning to beat him where the world could see, but the neighbor looked over the fence and cried out, "You will hurt him for all his life if you beat him for that!" And Christophilos' mother threw down the stick and started to quarrel with the neighbor instead, which was what he wanted.

The next morning the monk came riding back, and he had sold the wine, and Mavroula, the wild pig, and he had a fine, fat lamb on the saddle in front of him.

When she saw the lamb and the great crowd of villagers following the mule, the mother of Christophilos was proud and happy because no one else had a lamb.

She cried, "See what comes of being a virtuous, hardworking woman!" and she ran out of the house, and helped the monk off the mule and thanked him. She tied the lamb near the front door where all the world could see it; and the world came, and poked it in the ribs and said what a fine lamb it was. The children brought him flowers and grass to eat, and some brought him raisins, for he was the only lamb in the village.

—JOICE M. NANKIVELL

# The White Blackbird

"Oh, no, it cannot be," said all the creatures of the farmyard when the little wren told them what she had seen.

"Yes, yes, yes," said the little wren excitedly, "I flew and I fluttered along the hedges, and I saw it, just as I tell you."

"What did you see, O what did you see?" asked the foolish pigeons. They came to where the cock with the hens was standing, and they stretched out their necks to hear what was being said.

"Something too terrible to talk to foolish creatures about," said the cock as he went away.

"Too terrible, too terrible," said the robin redbreast mournfully, as she went hopping under the hedge.

Inside the house the boy was standing, and he was looking into a cage. Within that cage was a bird he had caught. It was the most wonderful of all birds, for it was a white blackbird. Now you might live a whole lifetime and never once see a white blackbird. But this boy had not only seen a white blackbird—he had caught one.

He had put the white blackbird into a cage, and he was going to keep it forever. It would be his very own. He was often lonely, this boy. His father and his mother had gone into another world, and he lived in the house of his grandmother, his mother's mother.

He had once, a long, long time ago, an elder brother who had lived in the house with him. But his brother had gone, and no one thought that he would be in that house again. For he had gone to be a soldier, and he had been away long, and no one had ever heard from him since he had gone. The boy, then, had no one to take him by the hand as other boys had. He used to tell his grandmother about seeing boys with their elder brothers, the boys holding their brothers' hands. But he had given up telling her about such sights, for she sighed when he talked about brothers together.

Now the boy had a bird for his very own. That was a joy to him. The night before he had been at an uncle's house. He came out of the barn with a man who carried a lantern. The man held the lantern into a bush. The light came upon a bird that was resting there. Dazzled by the light the bird did not move, and the man put his hand upon the bird, caught it, and gave it to the boy to keep. This was the white blackbird. The next day he carried the bird home.

He put the bird into an empty cage. Now that he had something of his own, he would not be lonely when he saw such and such a boy walking with his brother on the Easter Sunday that was coming. All day he watched the strange white bird. And that night as he sat by the fire his eyes were upon the cage, and he watched the stirring of the white blackbird within.

The robin redbreast that in the winter goes along under the hedge and the little wren that flies along the top of the hedge were talking to each other. "Always, on Easter Sunday," said the wren, "I sing my first song of the year. My first song is for the Risen Lord."

"And mine, too," said the robin redbreast. "But now we will not know that it is Easter morning and that it is time to sing for the

Risen Lord. For the white blackbird always showed itself to us in times before, and when it showed itself we knew it was Easter indeed."

"O now we know what has happened," said the foolish pigeons. "The boy has caught the white blackbird that used to appear just before the sun was up every Easter morning. He has brought the white blackbird into the house and he has put it into a cage. Now it will not be able to show itself. Dear, dear! We are truly sorry."

"The songs that the robin and the wren sing are not so very important," said the cock. "But think of the proclamation that I have made every Easter morning, *Mok an o-ee slaun,* 'the Son of the virgin is safe.' I made it when the white blackbird showed himself. Now men will not know that they may be rejoiceful."

"I—I" said the wren, looking around very bravely.

"The world will be the worse for not hearing my tidings," said the cock.

"I—I—" said the wren again.

"The wren is trying to say something, and no one will listen to her," said robin redbreast.

"Oh, by all means let the wren keep on talking," said the cock, and he went away.

"Tell us, tell us—" said the pigeons.

"I," said the little wren, "will try to set the white blackbird free."

"How, how—," said the foolish pigeons.

"I might fly into the house when no one is watching," said the wren. "I can really slip into and out of places without being seen. I might manage to open the door of the cage that the white blackbird is in."

"Oh, it is terrible in the house," said the foolish pigeons; "we went in once, picking grains. The door was closed on us. It was dark in there. And we saw the eyes of the cat watching us." Then the pigeons flew away.

"I should be afraid to go in," said the robin redbreast, "now that they have mentioned the eyes of the cat."

"I *am* afraid," said the little wren. "And there is no one that would miss me if anything befell me. I really am so afraid that I want to fly right away from this place."

But then, although her little heart was beating very fast, the wren flew up on the thatched porch. There was no one could see her there, so small and so brown she was. When darkness came outside she fluttered into the house. She hid in a corner of the dresser behind a little luster jug. She watched the cage that had the white blackbird in it. She saw the door of the house closed and bolted for the night.

Oh, all in a flutter was the little brown wren as she hid in one of the houses of men. She saw the cat sleeping by the hearth. She saw, when the fire burned low, how the cat rose and stretched herself, and looked all around the house with her eyes. The boy and his grandmother had now gone up to bed. The wren could still see by the light that blazed up on the hearth. The cat went up one step of the stairs. But only a step. For as the wren fluttered up and alighted on the top of the cage the cat heard the sound that she made, light and all as it was, and she turned back and looked at the cage, and the little wren knew that the cat saw her and would watch her.

There was a little catch on the door of the cage. The wren pulled at it. She said to the bird within, "O white messenger!"

"How will I fly out of the house? Tell me, tell me," said the white blackbird.

"We will fly up the chimney and away," said the little wren as she opened the door.

Before the darkness had quite gone a young man came along the road that went by that house. He had on the clothes of a soldier. He stood and looked at the house as he came before it. But he would not stay after he had looked upon it. His years of service in the army were over, but he would go on to the town and join the army again.

For he had joined the army and gone into the war against the wish of his mother and his grandmother. His mother he could never see again, and his grandmother he did not want to see. He had looked upon the house he was born in, and he would go on again.

It was near daylight now. Out of the hedge came a thin little song. It was the song of the wren, he knew, and he smiled as he listened to it. He heard another song, a song with joyous notes in it, the first song that the robin sings from the hedgetops. All the times before she had been going under the hedges without a song.

And then he heard the cock crow. Loudly, loudly, the cock cried, *"Mok an o-ee slaun, Mok an o-ee slaun,"* and when he heard that call the young man remembered that this was Easter morning. He did not go on now. He waited, and he stood looking at the house.

And then upon the thatch of the porch he saw a strange bird— a strange white bird. The young man could not go on now. Once only in a lifetime might one see a white blackbird. And this was the second time he had seen one. Once before, and on an Easter morning too, he had seen a white blackbird. He had come out of this house a little boy. His young mother was in it then. She had called him early in the morning, so that he might see the sun rise on Easter morning. And just as soon as he had gone outside he had seen a strange bird on the thatch of the porch—he had seen the white blackbird then as he saw it now.

He did not go. He remembered that there was a baby in the

house that would be a boy now—a boy such as he was when he had gone outside that Easter morning and had stood watching the bird and whispering to his mother so that she might not frighten it. And his mother had seen the white blackbird too, and she had told him about it being the messenger to the birds to tell them that it is Easter.

He did not go.

Then out of the house came a little boy. He held an empty cage in his hand. He looked all around. He saw the white blackbird upon the thatch of the porch, and he held his hands to the bird as if trying to draw it down to him.

The young man went to the boy. And the boy, knowing him, caught the hand that was held to him. The boy drew the young man within. There was an old woman at the hearth. She turned and saw the young man, and for a long time she remained looking on him.

"Safe, safe," cried the cock outside.

"And you are safe, my daughter's son," said the woman, "safe, thanks to the Risen Lord. And now this child will have a brother to take him by the hand this Easter."

The boy felt that never again would he have a lonely thought. His great brother was holding him by the hand. He heard the robin singing. He heard the wren singing. He heard the cock telling all the world about the Risen Lord. And without any sorrow he watched the white blackbird flying away.

—FROM *The Peep Show Man* BY

PADRAIC COLUM

# Merry Easter

José went slowly out the schoolroom door. He was puzzled. Just a few minutes before, Miss Martin had told the class, "We will have our Easter party after school next Friday. Will each of you please bring two colored eggs for the egg hunt?"

José wanted to ask his teacher to explain, but he was ashamed. He had asked so many questions since he came to the United States from Mexico six months ago. If only Miss Martin could explain things to him in Spanish. Then he wouldn't make so many mistakes! But school was over for the day.

Maybe Mama would know. José pushed back his straight black hair and started to run.

"Mamacita," he called, hurrying into the kitchen, "what do you know about the colored eggs which are used by the Americanos?"

Mama was patting corn meal into thin, round tortillas for their dinner. She smiled and shook her head. "José, you are an Americano now too. Why don't you ask your new friends to help you?"

José scowled. "No, I am a Mexican," he said. "And my friends are Manuel and Carmen at home in our village."

José thought of the games of huesitos he had played with

Manuel. He was very good at that. Not like these strange games called 2-square and tetherball they played here at school. He would never learn all the rules! Never!

And so many new words to remember. When he said "Happy Christmas," it was a mistake. So at Timmy Nelson's birthday party he was very careful to say "Merry Birthday." But that was wrong too! José thought of the gay birthday parties and fiestas he had gone to in Mexico. Everyone had danced and joked and played tricks on each other with cascarrones. They had been wonderful parties. His brown eyes sparkled.

"The colored eggs, Mama! Perhaps they are cascarrones! Maybe that is what Miss Martin wants us to bring."

His mother looked puzzled. "I have never heard of that custom in this country. And only two cascarrones each! Doesn't your teacher know that three or four would be much better?"

José clapped his hands. "Mama, let us make enough cascarrones for everyone. Then we will be able to surprise my teacher."

Mama laughed and said, "We will have to eat many eggs in order to have enough shells by next Friday. It is lucky we have a large family."

All week José, his father, and his little sisters seemed to eat nothing but eggs, eggs, and more eggs. Mama did not crack the eggs to open them. Instead, she made a small hole in one end with her sharp scissors and let the egg run into a dish. Then José carefully washed out the empty shell and let it drain dry.

The day before the party, José and his sisters painted the eggshells with water colors. They looked like a rainbow piled in a big earthenware bowl. That night Papa brought home a bag of confetti. He emptied the bag into a dish and everyone took turns pouring the tiny dots of brightly colored paper into the eggshells. When the

shells were nearly full, the ends were sealed with crepe paper and paste. How beautiful the cascarrones looked! José was pleased.

The next day José asked Miss Martin if he could hide something in the cloakroom. "It is a surprise for the party," he told her. He could hardly wait for the fun to begin.

At last it was time for the children to put all their eggs in a big basket so the room mother could hide them outdoors. José saw then that he had made another mistake. The other children's eggs were not cascarrones. They were boiled eggs, with coloring on them. The happy excitement in José's heart changed to an icy worried feeling in his stomach. If only he had asked Miss Martin what kind of eggs to bring!

José followed the others to the playground. Maybe, he thought, Miss Martin would forget about his surprise. But he couldn't take the cascarrones home—not after his whole family had worked so hard and eaten eggs all week.

He was too worried to really look for the eggs, and when the hunt was over, he had found only one. Who would expect to find an egg under a bush or on top of a fence post, anyway? He did not understand. Just then he heard Miss Martin say, "Boys and girls, José has a surprise for us. Will you get it, please, José?"

José carried the box out slowly. Everyone crowded around to see.

"Oh, just more eggs," someone said. Silently José gave three cascarrones to each person. Everyone thanked him politely, but said nothing more.

José thought of the fiestas in Mexico and all his laughing friends there. Didn't Americanos like to laugh and play tricks? They had taught him their games and to say the right words. Maybe he would have to teach them all the secret of the cascarrones.

José took a cascarrone and ran up to Timmy Nelson. For a minute he couldn't think of the right thing to say. Then he knew.

"Merry Easter, Timmy." José cried, and broke the cascarrone on top of Timmy's hair and clothes. The eggshell was so thin that it didn't hurt Timmy at all, but for a second he looked very much surprised.

Then Timmy began to laugh. He cracked a cascarrone on José's head and shouted, "Merry Easter, José!" Suddenly all the children were breaking cascarrones on each other's heads and shouting, "Merry Easter." They laughed to see the bright bits of paper scatter over themselves and on the grass like hundreds of tiny flowers. Miss Martin laughed too, "Oh, what a lovely surprise!"

For a moment it seemed to José just like fiesta time in Mexico. There were just as many friendly faces and laughing voices here. Maybe he could even teach Timmy to play huesitos sometime!

There was one cascarrone left. José hurried toward Timmy. I will tell him to call me Joe, the Americano, from now on, he thought. But first I will give him another little surprise—right on top of his head!

—NORA HUNTER

# Priapos of the Harbor

Now spring returning beckons the little boats
Once more to dance on the waters; the gray storms
Are gone that scourged the sea. Now swallows build
Their round nests in the rafters, and all the fields
Are bright with laughing green.
Come then, my sailors;
Loose your dripping hawsers, from their deep-sunk graves
Haul up your anchors, raise your brave new sails.
It is Priapos warns you, god of this harbor.

—ANTIPATER OF SIDON

176

# The Shout in the Valley

Here is a strange and wonderful tale that is said to have happened in ancient Britain at Easter in the year A.D. 429. It is told in an old, old manuscript, carefully written by hand in the eighth century. Perhaps you can find in your library a translation of this old, old book, Bede's *Ecclesiastical History of England.* If so, turn to Book I, Chapter 20, and read the story for yourself in the quaint words of long ago.

The Place: Open country in northeastern Wales, near the River Dee.

The Time: Easter season, 429 A.D.

The People: Germanus, a bishop who had been called from France to teach the ancient Britons. Lupus, a priest who traveled with Germanus. A boy and girl of Britain, friends of Germanus and Lupus. Other Britons—men, women, and children. A runner, quite out of breath. Picts and Saxons, armed and savage.

Germanus, Lupus, the boy and the girl enter slowly from the left. They are walking slowly, enjoying the first spring flowers and the singing of the birds.

177

Germanus: Shall we rest here a while? It has been a long walk. (The men sit on rocks; the children on the ground.)

Lupus: A long walk—but beautiful.

Girl: Oh, I am so happy! (The others look at her as though asking why.) There were larks singing in the meadow. I saw a daffodil in bloom by our cottage. The red buds and the green leaves are beginning to show on the trees.

Boy: I am happy for more than that.

Lupus: Why are you happy, my boy?

Boy: My heart is singing because you have come to teach us. If you had stayed in France, this would have been just one more spring-time in Britain. Because you came, it is *Easter.*

Girl: It is wonderful that we can still be happy about something that happened so long ago. It is four hundred years since that first Easter when people knew that Jesus lived.

Germanus: Four hundred years *is* a long time, my child. But, mark my word! The Christians of Britain will still be rejoicing at Easter time a thousand years from now—even two thousand years from now.

Lupus: I hope you speak the truth, Father Germanus. But right now it looks as though Christian Britons might not live to see the sun set on this Easter.

Boy: What do you mean, Father Lupus?

Lupus: There are bad rumors about the Picts and Saxons. They are fully armed and marching in hordes against us.

Germanus: I cannot believe that, Lupus. Anyway, I must hurry to my people. Many of them have gone ahead and are waiting by the river for us to baptize them. Others are on the way.

Lupus: We should leave some sort of sign here to show which path we have taken.

Boy: My sister and I will stay here to tell everyone which way to go.

Girl: Yes, let us stay.

Germanus: But you wanted to come with us!

Boy: This can be our Easter offering—waiting here instead of going on with you.

(Germanus places his hand on the boy's head, then the girl's in silent blessing. Germanus and Lupus go off at the right. The boy and the girl sit on the rocks. They sing softly:)

> A solis ortus cardine
> Ad usque terrae limitem
> Christum canamus principem
> Natum Maria virgine.

(They stop humming as they hear voices in the distance at the left. A group of Britons enter—men, women, and children.)

A Briton: Which way did the holy men go?

Boy: They turned to the right and followed the path to the river.

A Child of the Britons: We are going to the river to be baptized. That's the way we show that we want to be good.

(The group goes off to the right. The boy and girl sing again until another group appears at the left.)

Briton: Did Father Germanus and his friend pass this way?

Boy: They took the path at the right toward the river.

Briton: Aren't you going there, too?

Boy: Later.

(The Britons go off at the right. The boy and the girl start to sing but are interrupted by a voice shouting.)

: Germanus. Father Germanus.

(A runner appears from the left, panting for breath.)

Runner: Have you seen anyone pass?

Boy: Many have taken the path to the river.

Runner: The holy men too? (drops wearily down on stone to rest)

Boy: Yes. What is the matter? Why do you want them?

Runner: (breathing with difficulty) Bad news! Terrible news! The Picts and the Saxons are coming. They are almost here. They have their swords bared for battle.

Boy: I will call Father Germanus. You are too tired to run farther. I am rested, and I know the way. (Boy runs off at the right.)

Runner: (calling after boy) Bring Father Germanus here. I must tell him everything. I will follow you as soon as I can breathe again. (Girl disappears on left for a moment. She returns with water in a piece of bark. The runner drinks. Voices are heard at right. The boy, Germanus, and Lupus enter at right followed by Britons. They crowd at the entrance in a way that suggests there are many more behind them.)

Germanus: The Picts and Saxons? Where are they?

Runner: They follow the trail through the hills. (points back toward left) They will be here in a few minutes.

Germanus: Are there many?

Runner: There are many. Each one is a soldier with a sword flashing in his hands.

Briton: We are unarmed. There are but few of us. We are lost!

Girl: Father Germanus will think of a way to save us. (All murmur in panic, except Father Germanus and Lupus. They stand quiet and poised—thinking. Their calmness has its effect on the others. These stop murmuring. They look silently at the two priests.)

Germanus: (with a sudden smile) Do you remember the Easter song of praise we have been learning?

Britons: You mean "Alleluia"?

Germanus: It is a beautiful word—Alleluia. It is a word we can shout with all our might. (The others look at him blankly.)

Briton: But men are coming. They are coming soon—with swords. This is no time to sing praises to God. This is no time to shout Alleluia.

Germanus: It is always the time to praise God. It is always the time to shout Alleluia.

Briton: We can't waste time talking. We must *do* something.

Germanus: And this is what we can do.

All: Tell us.

Germanus: Do you all know the valley where the great oak grows? The valley that has hills on every side?

Boy: The Valley of Echoes?

Germanus: (smiling) Yes, the Valley of Echoes. We will go there and wait till the Picts and Saxons are almost upon us. We will wait till they are even in the Valley of Echoes with us. Watch me—all of you. When the right time comes, I will shout "Alleluia! Alleluia! Alleluia!" In that Valley of Echoes our praises to God will sound like the voice of a great army. Those who sing praises to God have a strength greater than their own. Come with me to the Valley of Echoes.

(All go out at right. Stage is empty for a minute. Then voices and clanging swords are heard approaching at left. A group of Picts and Saxons enter. Some stand at the entrance giving the impression that a great army is behind them.)

Leader of Picts and Saxons: There are many footprints here. They are fresh prints. What we heard must be true. The Britons are celebrating a Christian holy day called Easter. Come! Let us follow them.

(Soldiers start across the stage. They walk confidently. Some disappear at right. Others follow at intervals, giving the impression of more to come.)

Germanus: (in a loud and triumphant voice offstage) **Alleluia! Alleluia! Alleluia!**

All the Britons: (loudly offstage) Alleluia! Alleluia! Alleluia!

Echo: (offstage) Alleluia! Alleluia! Alleluia! Alleluia! Alleluia! Alleluia! Alleluia! Alleluia! Alleluia!

(Picts and Saxons who have gone off at right come stampeding back across stage. They drop their swords. They stumble over each other. They show terrible fright.)

Leader of Picts and Saxons: There are more of them than we thought.

There must be thousands. Their shouts come from the rocks on
every side. They are shouting from the skies themselves.
(Picts and Saxons disappear in confusion at left.)

Germanus: (triumphantly offstage) It is *always* the time to praise
God!

Echo:—to praise God!

Germanus: (triumphantly offstage) It is *always* the time to sing
Alleluia!

Echo—sing Alleluia!

Germanus: (offstage) Those who praise God have a strength greater
than their own!

Echo:—greater than their own!

—ALICE GEER KELSEY

# Candles at Midnight

Now that he was ten, Costas Papadopoulos remembered very little about that long-ago time when he was only five. He had little in common with the small boy who thought he was hungry if dinner was ten minutes late and who thought that soldiers were only for parades. But in spite of all Costas had learned about hunger and enemy soldiers during the last five years in Athens, there was one thing he did remember very clearly and very often. He could never forget the promises of the night before Easter, 1940.

"Next year you will be old enough to go," his father had promised him, speaking loudly because of the clanging of all the church bells of Athens. "It is enough this year for you to come up here on our flat roof at midnight to watch."

"And shall I have fireworks to set off?" Costas had asked. His eyes had sparkled at the red, green, and gold of the Roman candles and rockets hissing and popping from Mt. Lycabettus and other hills about Athens.

"We shall stand together on the highest rock of Mt. Lycabettus to fire our rockets," Kyrios Papadopoulos had promised his son.

"And shall I have a candle to carry?" Costas had asked. His

eyes danced from one place to another, as people at all churches in Athens were obeying the midnight bells and lighting their Easter candles. His eyes raised again to Mt. Lycabettus where the bell of St. George's chapel was ringing in triumph. The top of the mountain was blossoming in tiny golden flames as lights were passed from one candle to another. "Shall I have a long, white candle to carry from the top of Mt. Lycabettus?"

"Of course you will!" his mother had promised. "And you will shield it with your hand so carefully that it will stay lighted all the time that you walk the winding path down the mountain and through the streets home. That will bring you good luck all the year."

Four Easters had passed since then, but there had been no midnight fireworks nor long, white candles for Costas. The spring when Costas was six, his father had been in the Greek army fighting in the mountains. The Easters when he was seven and eight and nine, there had been conquering soldiers in Athens, insisting that each Greek be in his own house early every evening.

Now that Costas was ten, beautiful Athens was free again. Often during that sunny week before Easter, 1945, Costas had climbed the twisting stairway to his roof to get a better look at Mt. Lycabettus. At almost any time, he could see the tiny figures of people toiling up the hill to say their Holy Week prayers in the gleaming, whitewashed chapel of St. George at the summit.

"You are old enough to go alone now, Costas," his father said to him on the day before Easter.

"Yes, Father!" The boy understood why his father could not go with him. It had been four years now that Kyrios Papadopoulos had been out of the army and walking painfully with a cane. The long climb up Mt. Lycabettus would be hard for him at any time—quite impossible as part of the gay Easter crowd.

"I will watch from the roof," smiled the father. "Point your rockets over this house. Then I will know which are yours."

"All right," grinned Costas, who could feel the fireworks in his fingers already. "And the long, white candle—I will carry it carefully all the way down the mountain and through the streets. I will climb up to our roof and give it to you still burning."

"You can try, smiled his mother.

"I *will* do it!" said Costas. "And bring you good luck for a whole long year."

"I am sorry not to have more money for fireworks and candles for you." Kyrios Papadopoulos opened his thin picketbook and slowly counted out some worn paper money. "Two hundred drachmas is all we can possibly spare. That would have been plenty before the war. Prices are higher now. I hope it will be enough."

"You need spend nothing for Easter eggs." His mother pointed at the basket of bloodred eggs on the table. "You can carry two in your pocket. When the bells ring at midnight, you will want to crack eggs with the other boys."

"I will go to the market now to buy the candle and the fireworks." Costas was out the door and racing down the narrow street toward the wide streets, beyond which lay the marketplace. Not far from his house, he saw a man with a cart, selling candles.

"How much?" asked Costas.

"Fifty drachmas for the short brown ones. Two hundred drachmas for the long white ones," droned the candleseller.

"But the short ones would not burn all the way down Mt. Lycabettus!" wailed Costas.

"The long ones will—only two hundred drachmas," droned the candle seller. His eyes were already on a woman who looked as though she had more money.

"But then there would not be anything left for buying fireworks!" groaned Costas.

The candle seller shrugged his shoulders. He turned toward
the young woman who held out money for three long white candles.

Costas went slowly on. Perhaps if he went on toward the market
streets, candles would be cheaper. He passed a man standing on
the sidewalk holding a tray of fireworks.

"How much?" asked Costas.

"Fifty drachmas." The man pointed at some puny little fire-
crackers. "One hundred drachmas. One hundred and fifty. Two hundred." He pointed to fireworks that grew bigger with the bigger
prices. The one for two hundred was a beauty.

Costas shuffled slowly on toward the marketplace near the foot
of the ancient Acropolis. Some days he loved to gaze dreamily at
the stately Parthenon and the dainty Temple of Victory outlined
against the sky. But today he was wondering merely if, where there
were many salesmen, prices would be lower.

"How much?" he asked of candle salesmen with trays, with
baskets, with pushcarts.

"Fifty for the short brown ones. Two hundred for the long white
ones." The answer was always the same.

"How much?" Costas asked of the candle salesmen sitting at
tables beside the doors of churches.

"Fifty for the short brown ones. Two hundred for the long white
ones."

Costas soon found it did no good to explain to the candle sellers
that he had only two hundred drachmas with which he must buy
at least one rocket and a long white candle that would burn all the
time that it took him to climb down Mt. Lycabettus, walk to his own
house, and mount the stairs to his father's roof. The candle salesmen

were always busy selling to someone whose drachmas did not have to spread so far. Costas looked enviously at grimy bootblacks and ragged water boys who could earn money of their own to spend.

It was nearly dark when Costas carried a long, slim, newspaper-wrapped parcel into the one big room that was home for himself and his parents. Tired, he flung himself onto the bed, under the picture of his father in uniform, while his mother put the plain supper on the table. This was the last of the fast-day meals. At midnight, with the cracking of the bloodred Easter eggs, the feasting would begin. Tomorrow there would be roast lamb and Easter sweets.

"Did you find the candle and fireworks?" asked his mother.

"Yes." But Costas did not offer to unroll his long, slim parcel.

"I wish I could climb Mt. Lycabettus with you tonight." said his mother, laying crunchy chunks of dark brown bread at each place. "But you know how hard it is for your father to be lame. I will watch with him from the roof. I will wait with him for you to come up the stairs to us with the last flickers of your tall, white Easter candle."

"Yes, Mother." Costas fingered the parcel. He started to say something. Just then his mother whisked out into the courtyard to draw cool water for the table. Costas said nothing.

Supper over, he rested a while, his paper parcel clutched tightly.

"Ten o'clock," called his father. "It's time to get ready to start up Mt. Lycabettus. You will want plenty of time to go into the chapel before midnight."

Costas rubbed sleepy eyes. He staggered out into the courtyard where, with a gourd, he dipped water from a big barrel to pour over his head, his hands, his feet. It was already warm enough to begin saving wear on shoes.

Costas went back to the table in the one big room. He chose two large bloodred eggs to stuff in his trouser pockets. He lifted the long paper parcel carefully and started for the door.

"We will be up on the roof when the bells begin to ring at midnight," promised his mother. "We will be watching the fireworks and the candles till you come climbing up the stairs with your burning candle."

Costas stood in the doorway as though there was something he wanted to say. He turned his long parcel slowly in his hand. He cleared his throat—but all that came was, "Good-bye, Father. Good-bye, Mother." He turned and went out alone into the night.

Costas had climbed Mt. Lycabettus often in the daytime, but never before in the middle of the night. He dodged through one dark, narrow street after another until one street ended in a long flight of stone steps. Then a turn to the left and he was on the broad road which hairpinned through the pines for the lower stretches of the trail up the mountainside. Then he turned off onto the path that zigzagged back and forth between the giant cactus plants, ascending little by little the steep sides of Lycabettus.

He could not leap ahead at his own speed because the path was filled with people climbing slowly, up and up. This gave more time to look down at the twinkling lights of the sprawling city. Where the loop made broad spots in the trail, salesmen of candles and fireworks had set up their little tables. Costas stopped by one and watched a bent little woman buy a short brown candle. He stopped by the next one and saw a well-dressed man count out two hundred drachmas for a tall white candle. He noticed that the fireworks were practically all sold out. He shifted his paper parcel to his other hand and climbed on up the looping path.

At the top of the mountain, he wriggled through the crowd

around the door of the chapel. Inside there were soft lights burning before sacred pictures. The long-haired priest in his black robes was chanting with the choir while people moved quietly in and out of the chapel. Everywhere was the thick fragrance of incense.

Costas did not linger long. He wanted to be on top of the highest point of Mt. Lycabettus when the midnight bells should announce that Easter had arrived. He went outside and climbed the high wall that edged the enclosure east of the chapel. He could look down at the lights of all Athens and Piraeus. He could see even the twinkle of the big lanterns on fishermen's boats out in the harbor.

Mt. Hymettus rose dark behind him. Gleaming golden over the city were the ancient temples of the Acropolis, now bathed in floodlights in honor of Holy Week. Above him, the stars seemed almost close enough to touch.

Far below, the deep bell of the great Metropolitan Church rang out clearly. It was midnight. All over the city, bells sprang to life. A joyous clanging rose from all the churches, celebrating at once the Resurrection of their Lord and the new freedom of their country. So thrilled was Costas with the triumphant chorus of bells that he quite forgot to break his bloodred eggs on those of the boys standing near him. It was only the snapping and hissing of fireworks and the lighting of candles that reminded him that he, too, had a part in the celebration.

He discarded the newspaper wrapping and stood looking at his treasures—a long and beautiful rocket and a short brown candle. He looked in shame at the little candle made of the cheap dark tallow which burned so quickly.

"If I do not light it until I am almost home, they will never know," he tried to comfort himself. But the plan that had seemed all right in the marketplace seemed all too shabby under the stars, with the bells ringing joyously all about him, and the people singing with the priest the praises of the Risen Lord.

Fireworks were going off on every side, with people dodging them and laughing excitedly. Children were cracking eggs together, each trying to prove his the stronger egg. In an attempt to forget the smallness of his brown candle, Costas raised his rocket high over his head. He lighted a match that sputtered and went out. He struck a second match. He almost touched it to the rocket—but paused.

All around the people were lighting their tall white candles for the march home. As long as the rocket was unspent, there was still a chance to change his mind. He listened to the bells of triumph. He heard the people chanting, "Christ is risen. He is risen indeed."

Costas held the rocket high over his head. In a small voice that could scarcely be heard for the shouting about him, he called, "Rocket for sale. Skyrocket for sale. Two hundred drachmas."

"I'll take it," said a voice close by. "I tried to buy some for my little Yiannis on the way here, but they were all sold."

Costas clung to his beautiful rocket for a moment. Then he handed it over, lingeringly, to the tall man who counted out four fifty-drachma notes.

"Would you mind," asked Costas in a tight, thin voice, "letting me stand near by while Yiannis sets off the rocket?"

The rocket sputtered and sailed high over the heads of the crowd. As it flickered out, Costas' eyes were drawn by candle processions around other churches far below in the city. Then, grasping his two hundred drachmas in his hand, Costas wriggled his way through the crowd to the table by the chapel door where candles were sold.

"A long white candle," called Costas, laying down the four crumpled fifty-drachma notes with a glad flourish.

The candle seller picked from the tray a candle that was truly beautiful in its tall, slim whiteness. The black-robed priest himself, smiling through his curly black beard, stooped to light Costas' candle. From the white candle, Costas lighted his short brown one. He pushed his way into the little chapel and placed a small candle before a picture of the Virgin Mary and the baby Jesus.

Then, proudly, Costas joined the happy throng that was chanting its way down the mountainside, each person carrying a lighted candle.

"Christ is risen!" they greeted each other.

"He is risen indeed!" was the answer.

Costas did not care if the procession was slow. Wasn't his the longest, whitest candle ever carried by a boy on an Easter midnight? It would surely burn for every stately step down the mountainside and for the quick walk through the narrow dark streets to his own home.

Singing and carrying his candle high, Costas pushed open his courtyard gate. One inch of candle left! Singing louder, he climbed the winding iron stairs to the roof. Three-quarters of an inch of candle left! The flame breathed hotly on his fingers as he crossed the roof to where his father sat. Half an inch of burning candle he thrust into his father's waiting hands.

"Christ is risen!" greeted Costas.

"He is risen indeed!" answered his parents.

—ALICE GEER KELSEY

# Joy Is Everywhere

At Alexander Burger J.H.S. 139, a large school in the city of New York, some of the students named as among their favorite poems the six which follow here. Even though these boys and girls now live in big housing projects in New York, their parents and some of the students themselves have come from other places and from a variety of national and racial backgrounds. The poems they chose are liked by girls and boys, men and women, everywhere. Besides the six in this group many other poems were selected by the students, but because of space limitations it has not been possible to include all of them. Among their other selections, appearing elsewhere in this book, are "Spring" by William Blake "The Coming of Spring" by Norah Perry; "Spring Grass" by Walt Whitman; "April Rain Song" by Langston Hughes; "Out in the Fields," author unknown; and "A Prayer in Spring" by Robert Frost.

# Spring Song

A bluebell springs upon the ledge,
A lark sits singing in the hedge;
Sweet perfumes scent the balmy air,
And life is brimming everywhere.
What lark and breeze and bluebell sing
  Is Spring, Spring, Spring!

No more the air is sharp and cold;
The planter wends across the wold,
And, glad, beneath the shining sky
We wander forth, my love and I;
And ever in our hearts doth ring
This song of Spring, Spring!

—LINES FROM *"Spring Song"*

BY PAUL LAURENCE DUNBAR

# Spring's Arrival

All the birds have come again,
Hear the happy chorus!
Robin, bluebird, on the wing,
Thrush and wren this message bring.
Spring will soon come marching in,
Come with joyous singing.

—FOLK POEM FROM GERMANY

# The Children's Song

The swallow has come again
Across the wide, white sea;
She sits and sings through the falling rain,
"O March, my beloved March!
And thou, sad February,
Though still you may cover with snow the plain,
You yet smell sweet of the Spring!"

—FOLK POEM FROM GREECE

197

# May Day

*(Oxfordshire Children's May Song)*

Spring is coming, spring is coming,
  Birdies, build your nest;
Weave together straw and feather,
  Doing each your best.

Spring is coming, spring is coming,
  Flowers are coming too:
Pansies, lilies, daffodillies,
  Now are coming through.

Spring is coming, spring is coming,
  All around is fair;
Shimmer and quiver on the river,
  Joy is everywhere.
  We wish you a happy May.

—AUTHOR UNKNOWN

# The Rhodora

In May, when sea-winds pierced our solitudes,
I found the fresh Rhodora in the woods,
Spreading its leafless blooms in a damp nook,
To please the desert and the sluggish brook.
The purple petals, fallen in the pool,
Made the black water with their beauty gay;
Here might the redbird come his plumes to cool,
And court the flower that cheapens his array.

Rhodora! if the sages ask thee why
This charm is wasted on the earth and sky,
Tell them, dear, that if eyes were made for seeing,
Then Beauty is its own excuse for being:
Why thou were there, O rival of the rose!
I never thought to ask, I never knew:
But, in my simple ignorance, suppose
The self-same Power that brought me there brought you.

—RALPH WALDO EMERSON

# May Is Building Her House

May is building her house. With apple blooms
  She is roofing over the glimmering rooms;
Of the oak and the beech hath she builded its beams,
  And, spinning all day at her secret looms,
With arras of leaves each wind-sprayed wall
She pictureth over, and peopleth it all
  With echoes and dreams,
  And singing of streams.

May is building her house. Of petal and blade
Of the roots of the oak, is the flooring made,
  With a carpet of mosses and lichen and clover,
  Each small miracle over and over,
And tender, traveling green things strayed.

Her windows, the morning and evening star,
And her rustling doorways, ever ajar
  With the coming and going
  Of fair things blowing,
And thresholds of the four winds are.

May is building her house. From the dust of things
She is making the songs and the flowers and the wings;
  From October's tossed and trodden gold
  She is making the young year out of the old;
    Yea: out of winter's flying sleet
    She is making all the summer sweet,
  And the brown leaves spurned of November's feet
She is changing back again to spring's.

—RICHARD LE GALLIENNE

# The Ratcatcher's Daughter

Once upon a time there lived an old ratcatcher who had a daughter, the most beautiful girl that had ever been born. Their home was a dirty little cabin; but they were not so poor as they seemed, for every night the ratcatcher took the rats he had cleared out of one house and let them go at the door of another, so that on the morrow he might be sure of a fresh job.

His rats got quite to know him and would run to him when he called; people thought him the most wonderful ratcatcher and could not make out how it was that a rat remained within reach of his operations.

Now anyone can see that a man who practiced so cunning a roguery was greedy beyond the intentions of Providence. Everyday, as he watched his daughter's beauty increase, his thoughts were: "When will she be able to pay me back for all the expense she has been to me?" He would have grudged her the very food she ate, if it had not been necessary to keep her in the good looks which were some day to bring him his fortune. For he was greedier than any gnome after gold.

Now all good gnomes have this about them: they love whatever is beautiful and hate to see harm happen to it. A gnome who lived far away underground below where stood the ratcatcher's house, said to his fellows: "Up yonder is a man who has a daughter; so greedy is he, he would sell her to the first comer who gave him gold enough! I am going up to look after her."

So one night, when the ratcatcher set a trap, the gnome went and got himself caught in it. There in the morning, when the ratcatcher came, he found a funny little fellow, all bright and golden, wriggling and beating to be free.

"I can't get out!" cried the little gnome. "Let me go!"

The ratcatcher screwed up his mouth to look virtuous. "If I let you out, what will you give me?"

"A sack full of gold," answered the gnome, "just as heavy as myself—not a pennyweight less!"

"Not enough!" said the ratcatcher. "Guess again!"

"As heavy as you are!" cried the gnome, beginning to plead in a thin, whining tone.

"I'm a poor man," said the ratcatcher. "A poor man mayn't afford to be generous!"

"What is it you want of me?" cried the gnome.

"If I let you go," said the ratcatcher, "you must make me the richest man in the world!" Then he thought of his daughter: "Also you must make the king's son marry my daughter; then I will let you go."

The gnome laughed to himself to see how the trapper was being trapped in his own avarice as, with the most melancholy air, he answered: "I can make you the richest man in the world; but I know of no way of making the king's son marry your daughter, except one."

"What way?" asked the ratcatcher.

"Why," answered the gnome, "for three years your daughter must come and live with me underground, and by the end of the third year her skin will be changed into pure gold like ours. And do you know any king's son who would refuse to marry a beautiful maiden who was pure gold from the sole of her foot to the crown of her head?"

The ratcatcher had so greedy an inside that he could not believe in any king's son refusing to marry a maiden of pure gold. So he clapped hands on the bargain and let the gnome go.

The gnome went down into the ground and fetched up sacks and sacks of gold until he had made the ratcatcher the richest man in the world. Then the father called his daughter, whose name was Jasomé and bade her follow the gnome down into the heart of the earth.

It was all in vain that Jasomé begged and implored; the ratcatcher was bent on having her married to the king's son. So he pushed, and the gnome pulled, and down she went; and the earth closed after her.

The gnome brought her down to his home under the hill upon which stood the town. Everywhere round her were gold and precious stones; the very air was full of gold dust, so that when she remained still it settled on her hands and her hair, and a soft golden down began to show itself over her skin. So there in the house of the gnome sat Jasomé and cried; and far away overhead, she heard the days come and go, by the sound of people walking and the rolling of wheels.

The gnome was very kind to her; nothing did he spare of underground commodities that might afford her pleasure. He taught her the legends of all the heroes that have gone down into earth and been forgotten and the lost songs of the old poets and the buried languages that once gave wisdom to the world; down there all these are remembered.

She became the most curiously accomplished and wise maiden that ever was hidden from the light of day. "I have to train you," said the gnome, "to be fit for a king's bride!" But Jasomé, though she thanked him, only cried to be let out.

In front of the ratcatcher's house rose a little spring of salt water with gold dust in it that gilded the basin where it sprang. When he saw it, he began rubbing his hands with delight, for he guessed well enough that his daughter's tears had made it; and the dust in it told him how surely now she was being turned into gold.

And now the ratcatcher was the richest man in the world; all his traps were made of gold, and when he went rathunting he rode in a gilded coach drawn by twelve hundred of the finest and largest rats. This was for an advertisement of the business. He now caught rats for the fun of it and the show of it, but also to get money for it; for though he was so rich, ratting and money-grubbing had become a second nature to him; unless he were at one or the other, he could not be happy.

Far below, in the house of the gnome, Jasomé sat and cried. When the sound of the great bells ringing for Easter came down to her, the gnome said; "Today I cannot bind you; it is the great rising day for all Christians. If you wish, you may go up and ask your father now to release you."

So Jasomé kissed the gnome and went up the track of her own tears, that brought her to her father's door. When she came to the light of day, she felt quite blind; a soft yellow tint was all over her, and already her hair was quite golden.

The ratcatcher was furious when he saw her coming back before her time. "Oh, father," she cried, "let me come back for a little while to play in the sun!" But her father, fearing lest the gilding of her complexion should be spoiled, drove her back into the earth, and trampled it down over her head.

The gnome seemed quite sorry for her when she returned; but already, he said, a year was gone—and what were three years, when a king's son would be the reward?

At the next Easter he let her go again; and now she looked quite golden, except for her eyes and her white teeth and the nails on her pretty little fingers and toes. But again her father drove her back into the ground, and put a heavy stone slab over the spot to make sure of her.

At last the third Easter came, and she was all gold.

She kissed the gnome many times and was almost sorry to leave him, for he had been very kind to her. And now he told her about her father catching him in the trap and robbing him of his gold by a hard bargain, and of his being forced to take her down to live with him, till she was turned into gold, so that she might marry the king's son. "For now," said he, "you are so compounded of gold that only the gnomes could rub it off you."

So this time, when Jasomé came up once more to the light of day, she did not go back again to her cruel father, but went and sat by the roadside and played with the sunbeams and wondered when the king's son would come and marry her.

And as she sat there all the country people who passed by stopped and mocked her; and boys came and threw mud at her because she was all gold from head to foot—an object, to be sure, for all simple folk to laugh at. So presently, instead of hoping, she fell to despair, and sat weeping with her face hidden in her hands.

Before long the king's son came along that road and saw something shining like sunlight on a pond. But when he came near, he found a lovely maiden of pure gold lying in a pool of her own tears, with her face hidden in her hair.

Now the king's son, unlike the countryfolk, knew the value of gold, but he was grieved at heart for a maiden so stained all over with it, and more, when he beheld how she wept. So he went to lift her up, and there, surely, he saw the most beautiful face he could ever have dreamed of. But, alas! so discolored—even her eyes and her lips and the very tears she shed were the color of gold! When he could bring her to speak, she told him how, because she was all gold, all the people mocked at her, and boys threw mud at her; and she

had nowhere to go, unless it were back to the kind gnome who lived underground, out of sight of the sweet sun.

So the prince said, "Come with me, and I will take you to my father's palace, and there nobody shall mock you, but you shall sit all your days in the sunshine, and be happy."

And as they went, more and more he wondered at her great beauty—so spoiled that he could not look at her without grief—and was taken with increasing wonder at the beautiful wisdom stored in her golden mind; for she told him the tales of the heroes which she had learned from the gnome, and of buried cities; also the songs of old poets that have been forgotten; and her voice, like the rest of her, was golden.

The prince said to himself, "I shut my eyes and am ready to die loving her, yet, when I open them, she is but a talking statue!"

One day he said to her, "Under all this disguise you must be the most beautiful thing upon earth! Already to me you are the dearest!" and he sighed, for he knew that a king's son might not marry a figure of gold.

Now one day after this, as Jasomé sat alone in the sunshine and cried, the little old gnome stood before her, and said. "Well, Jascmé, have you married the king's son?"

"Alas!" cried Jasomé, "you have so changed me: I am no longer human! Yet he loves me, and, but for that, he would marry me."

"Dear me!" said the gnome. "If that is all, I can take the gold off you again, why, I said so!"

Jasomé entreated him, by all his former kindness, to do so for her now.

"Yes," said the gnome, "but a bargain is a bargain. Now is the time for me to get back my bags of gold. Do you go to your father and let him know that the king's son is willing to marry you if he restores to me my treasure that he took from me, for that is what it comes to."

Up jumped Jasomé and ran to the ratcatcher's house. "Oh, father," she cried, "now you can undo all your cruelty to me, for now if you will give back the gnome his gold, he will give my own face back to me, and I shall marry the king's son!"

But the ratcatcher was filled with admiration at the sight of her and would not believe a word she said. "I have given you your dowry," he answered. "Three years I had to do without you to get it. Take it away and get married, and leave me the peace and plenty I have so hardly earned!"

Jasomé went back and told the gnome. "Really," said he, "I must show this ratcatcher that there are other sorts of traps and that it isn't only rats and gnomes that get caught in them! I have given him a taste of wealth; now it shall act as pickle to his poverty!"

So the next time the ratcatcher put his foot out of doors, the ground gave way under it, and snap—the gnome had him by the leg.

"Let me go!" cried the ratcatcher. "I can't get out!"

"Can't you?" said the gnome. "If I let you out, what will you give me?"

"My daughter!" cried the ratcatcher, "my beautiful golden daughter!"

"Oh, no!" laughed the gnome. "Guess again!"

"My own weight in gold!" cried the ratcatcher, in a frenzy; but the gnome would not close the bargain till he had wrung from the ratcatcher the promise of his last penny.

So the gnome carried away all the sacks of gold before the ratcatcher's eyes; and when he had them safe underground, then at last he let the old man go. Then he called Jasomé to follow him, and she went down willingly into the black earth.

For a whole year the gnome rubbed and scrubbed and tubbed her to get the gold out of her composition; and when it was done, she was the most shiningly beautiful thing you ever set eyes on.

When she got back to the palace, she found her dear prince pining for love of her and wondering when she would return. So they were married the very next day; and the ratcatcher came to look on at the wedding.

He grumbled because he was in rags and because he was poor; he wept that he had been robbed of his money and his daughter. But gnomes and daughters, he said, were in one and the same box; such ingratitude as theirs no one could beat.

—LAURENCE HOUSMAN

# How the Little Owl's Name Was Changed
## (*An Alaskan Folktale*)

Every spring in Alaska a little owl would come north with the other birds. It was a tiny owl and flew noiselessly over the tundra on its soft, downy wings. At first the Eskimos called him Anipausigak, which meant "the little owl." Later, after the Eskimos knew more about the bird, they called him Kerayule, which means in their language "the owl that makes no noise when he flies."

In the very early days before the white men came to Alaska, the Eskimos had no matches and it was very difficult for them to have a fire. Also there was very little wood in the Eskimo country.

One spring there was one family living all by themselves who had a bit of fire, but there was no place where they could get any if this went out. In the middle of the igloo was a pit, or hole, in the floor. Here a tiny little fire was kept burning at all times. Always someone watched it and tended it. The smoke went curling out of the window in the top of the igloo.

In this igloo were a little boy and a little girl with their mother and father. All times of the day and night someone had to stay in the house and watch the tiny fire. One day when the little girl was all alone—her folks were out hunting seals—some bad people came to the igloo.

"Oh, so you are all alone, little girl," one of them said. "I suppose you are watching the fire so that it does not go out?"

"Yes," said the little girl. "It would be very bad if we lost our fire. We would be very cold and would have nothing to cook by. I must watch it carefully so that when my parents come home there will be a warm house here to greet them."

The bad man laughed. "You will not have to watch your fire any more, little girl, for we have no fire in our igloo and we are going to take yours with us."

How frightened the little girl was and how badly she felt to think she was going to lose the fire! She thought quickly. "Can't I make you some fire on another stick, Mr. Man?" she asked. "Then you can take it with you and I will still have some left for my mother and father and my little brother when they come home from hunting seals."

"I haven't time to wait for you to make a new fire," the bad man said, "and, besides, I do not care if you are cold and hungry." With that he grabbed the fire and went away with it, leaving the poor little girl crying and all her fire gone.

When the mother and father and little brother came home they found the igloo cold, and the little girl told them what had happened. Hastily the father took his bow and arrow and set out to the igloo of the bad men to get his fire. When he got there, however, he found there were two men who guarded the fire day and night. They were big men and had big spears, and bows and arrows, too. So the poor man could not get his fire away from them. He begged them to let him have just a little of it to carry back to his wife and children, but they only laughed at him.

So for several days the good Eskimos had a terrible time. It was very cold, and they could not make a fire with anything. At last, one night, the father Eskimo thought of a plan. He called for the little owl Kerayule who makes no noise when he flies.

"Please, little owl, will you help us?" the Eskimo asked him. "You see we have no fire, and we are cold. Please, will you get our fire back for us from the bad men who took it away?"

"How can I do that?" asked the little owl. "I would like to help you, but they have spears and bows and arrows. Besides, they are much stronger than I am. Just how do you think I could get the fire?"

"You make no noise when you fly," the Eskimo man replied. "They will not hear you coming in the night. Also you can see in the darkness, and you can go straight to their igloo. The window in the top of it will be open, and you can look in and see how you can get the fire for us."

"I never thought of that," said the little owl. "I think, maybe, I can get the fire for you. I can see in the darkness, and I make no noise at all when I fly."

So the little owl set off through the dark night to the igloo where the bad men lived.

Carefully the owl flew over the igloo, and he did not make a sound. He looked into the window in the top where the smoke came out. He saw the fire—just one small stick burning in the fire pit. Also he saw one of the bad men sitting by it. He seemed to be asleep. The little owl hovered lower and alighted without a sound on the edge of the window. Silently, like a great soft feather, the little owl fluttered down into the igloo.

Right by the fire pit the little owl landed on the floor and the man did not see him. Maybe he was asleep, but the owl was not sure. Hopping softly across to the stick of fire, the little owl took the unburned end in his mouth and, with a great flutter, flew straight up through the open window in the top of the igloo. As he did, the man awakened. He grabbed his bow and arrow to shoot the little owl but was too late. Out into the night sailed the little owl, through the black darkness. He flew straight to the igloo of the good Eskimos.

The children were watching for the little owl, and soon they saw the fire come flying through the black sky. "Look!" shouted the little girl. "See the sparkling fire coming!"

And to this day the Eskimos at Hooper Bay call the little owl "sparkling fire owl" or, in their language, Kennreirk. Sometimes in the spring, when the sparkling fire owl comes to Hooper Bay and hovers around, the people will listen closely to see if they can hear him make any noise. Sometimes—very rarely—he makes a little snapping with his beak or a flutter with his wings. If the people can hear him make any noise they are very glad, for that is the best of good omens. They say the little sparkling fire owl is sending them good luck. If they go hunting they are sure to get a seal, or an eider duck, or a fat fish.

The Eskimo people love the little sparkling fire owl because he brings them good luck, and, too, when they see him they know the springtime has come to stay.

—CHARLES E. GILLHAM

# Karma's Holiday

Karma sat on the doorstep slowly spinning her top on the street. The top spun steadily and stayed in an upright position, but Karma did not care. A week before she had been proud of the top. She had made it from a long matchstick which someone had thrown away. When a street waterer had gone by throwing a fine spray of water from his goatskin onto the dusty street, Karma had rolled the matchstick around in the mud. She had held it carefully as she rolled it, shaping it evenly all around. When it was dry, she found that it spun better than any top she had ever seen.

But today the pride in her top was gone. Karma could think of nothing but *Shem en Naseem,* the spring holiday on which everyone went out to "Smell the Breezes."

For every spring holiday that Karma could remember up to this time, she had had a new dress. Right now, Karma was wearing the dress which she had worn on *Shem en Naseem* the year before. It had been a very pretty dress when it was new, but now it was faded and worn. She didn't see how she could enjoy walking along the streets to the gardens in such an old dress, while other people were wearing bright new clothes.

Just then Karma's friend Suad came skipping along the street. "Come and play hopscotch!" she called to Karma, as she went toward a group of children who were playing together a little farther down the street.

Karma got up and walked slowly toward the children. She usually enjoyed these street games, but today she felt so disappointed about the coming holiday that good times did not seem inviting.

After Karma had been with the children a little while her mother came to the door of their house and called, "Karma! Where are you? Come and take care of your brother. If no one watches him, he might fall into the fire while I cook dinner."

Karma returned to her house with shuffling steps. She was pouting and looked very unhappy. Her mother knew what the trouble was, and said, "Why are you acting this way? Such a fuss over a new dress!"

"But every other year I have had a new dress for spring holiday!"

"Can't you understand that business has been very bad, and your father has no money for new clothes? Come now and take care of your brother." The mother placed the baby astride Karma's hip and went back into the house.

The baby began to cry, and Karma slapped him on the back, saying, "Be quiet." Then she jiggled him up and down till he was quiet. After a while Karma saw her father turn the corner on his way home for dinner. She ran toward him and said, "O my father, have you thought of any way you could get me a dress for *Shem en Naseem*?"

"Hush, my child. These are unsettled days in Egypt. Until things are quiet tourists will not come and buy my pieces of carved ivory. We are lucky to have food to eat."

"Father, let me go to the shop this afternoon. I will bring you good luck."

"Well," said her father, "I see no reason why you should not come. You will see that the shop is full of beads and pins, carved ornaments and inlaid boxes, but no customers."

By this time they had reached the houses. They went in and sat on the floor around the pot of vegetable stew which the mother had prepared. Each member of the family broke off a piece of the flat round bread and dipped it into the stew. They ate noisily and did no talking until they had finished. Then Karma said, "Mother, I am going back to the shop with father this afternoon. I hope I will bring him luck."

The father nodded and said to the mother, "At the shop Karma will see why I am not able to buy new dresses for the holiday."

"Never mind," the mother said to him. "I can wash our dresses. We will send them out to the ironer on Sunday, and they will be fresh for Monday morning."

"But my old, worn-out dress!" wailed Karma. "All the other girls have new dresses."

"Be quiet! Stop worrying your father," the mother said.

After dinner Karma's father lay down on the sofa and went to sleep. Although it was still early in spring, the air was hot in the middle of the day. Shops were closed and locked while people took afternoon rest. Karma took her baby brother up the stairs and walked across the flat roof to the bedroom in which all the family slept. She pulled a mattress out from under the bed and lay down on it next to her brother. Soon both were asleep.

She woke with a start as her father called, "Karma! Hurry up if you want to go with me."

Grabbing the baby, Karma ran downstairs and gave him to

her mother. "You will see," she said. "I will bring luck to the shop and perhaps Father will be able to buy cloth for a dress."

Her mother sighed. "Don't you know it's too late to get a dress made now, even if he could buy material? All the dressmakers already have too much work, getting dresses ready for the holiday."

But Karma ran off hopefully with her father. When they reached the shop he unlocked the folding metal door which went across the front, folded it back at one side, and they walked in. "If you are careful, you may dust the carvings," he said.

Karma walked to the small showcase and clapped her hands in delight as she looked at the figures within. "There is the elephant with the raised trunk! I'm glad no one has bought him," she said. "Long may it remain to bring you good luck."

"It would be better luck to sell it and have some money," grumbled her father. He took off his coat and tarboosh and sat down at a worktable in the back of the small shop.

Karma took a rag and went behind the showcase. First she took out her favorite elephant, dusted it, and then put it back. Then she chose a small wooden box inlaid with ivory and mother of pearl. After that she dusted the carved beads, pins, paper knives, several vases, and the carved animals. "But where is the beautiful inlaid tray, Father?" she asked.

"I have put it away to keep it safe until things get better," he replied. "If no one will buy these little things, who would buy a valuable tray?"

"But I like to see the tray and turn it in the light to watch the pearl sparkle!" Karma said.

Just then someone called into the shop from the open doorway. "You, Habeeb! Come, have a cup of coffee." It was a friend of Karma's father—a man who kept another shop next door.

"Thank you," answered the father. "I will come. Karma, watch the shop."

"May I take care of the customers?"

"Customers?" said Habeeb as he went out. "There has been no customer in this shop for five days."

After he had gone, Karma continued dusting and rearranging articles in the showcase. She was busy when a shadow fell across the light from the doorway. Karma looked up. Two women were coming in. They were Egyptians, but were dressed like Europeans. "They must have enough money to buy something," thought Karma. She laid, "Welcome, ladies."

"Greetings to you," answered one of the women. "Where is the shopkeeper?"

"My father will be here soon. What do you wish to see?"

The women looked at the carvings in the showcase and asked to see some ivory and ebony candlesticks. After looking at them, one of the women said to the other, "I hoped we could find something a little more unusual than these items. Let's try another shop."

"Wait!" begged Karma. "My father has beautiful things put away. One is the most beautiful tray in all the town." She ran to the doorway and shouted, "Father! Come quickly, my father!"

Habeeb came from his friend's shop, grumbling, "What is the matter, troublesome girl?"

Karma pulled him toward the door. "Show the ladies your inlaid try," she urged. "Show them the beautiful tray."

Habeeb hurried and greeted the customers. "Good day. You are welcome. Sit down, if you please." He pulled up a bench for them. Then he went to the back of the room, unlocked a cupboard and brought out a round tray which he dusted and held up to the light. The tray was made of wood, inlaid with many small pieces of ivory and mother-of-pearl. In the center a design of wood was showing. Holding up the tray so the light shone on the mother-of-pearl, Habeeb turned it to show sparkling changes of color.

"It is beautiful," said one of the women.

"How much do you want for it?" asked the other.

"There is no other tray like it anywhere," said Karma's father. "It took many days to make it. But since you like it I will let you have it for three pounds."

"Three pounds!" cried the woman who had asked the price. "One pound is plenty."

"One pound!" cried Habeeb. "You must be joking! Karma, show them an inlaid box. They don't appreciate a valuable tray like this." The shopkeeper took the tray as if to put it away, then turned and added, "I will lose money but perhaps, for you only, I will sell it for two pounds and a half."

"Do you think we have money to throw away?" asked one woman. "We cannot pay more than a pound and a half."

The women turned as if leaving, but Karma cried, "Ladies, please buy the tray! Then I can have a new dress for *Shem en Naseem!*"

One woman answered. "So, your daughter has no dress for the holiday, yet you refuse to sell your tray at the right price."

"Never mind," said Habeeb, "I will sell my tray for a good price. But it is Saturday, too late for my daughter to get a dress made even if I buy the cloth."

"You can take her to the new store on Station Street," one woman said. "There they sell ready-made dresses. For her sake, we will give you two pounds for the tray, but not one piaster more!"

"Alas! I lose money, but for the sake of my daughter I will take two pounds."

The women gave him the money, and he gave them the tray. As they left one woman said to Karma," Go home, get washed, and put on shoes before you go to the new shop. We hope you have a very happy holiday on Monday."

Karma was jumping up and down from happiness. "Come, Father, let us go home and then to that shop!"

Habeeb locked the shop door and walked home after Karma, who was flying along. When she reached the house she called, "Oh, Mother, I must wash my hair and bathe and put on my sandals. I'm going to the new shop to buy a dress. Just ask father!"

"Habeeb, have you lost your mind, too?" asked the mother.

"Get Karma ready. She helped me sell the inlaid tray, and the customers told us where to buy a dress ready-made."

Karma's mother brought a bowl of water. Karma bathed and dressed. She washed her hair, braided it in two tight braids and tied a kerchief around her head. Then she hurried with her father to the new shop.

Never before had they seen such a store. Everything was clean and arranged on shelves, in showcases, and on hangers. A clerk found two dresses which were the right size for Karma. When she put on the first one, Karma exclaimed with delight and begged, "Please buy this one."

Her father said to the clerk, "You must offer it at a good price."

"There is only one price for each article in this shop," said the clerk. "We do not bargain."

"I never heard of such a thing! How do you manage to get any business?" inquired Habeeb. When the clerk told him the price of the dress, he realized it was fair, yet he wished he could have bargained and gotten it for less. However, for Karma's sake he took the dress.

When they reached home, she could hardly wait to show the dress to her mother. She was pleased that her mother liked the dress, and she wished her mother had a new one too. Then Karma ran quickly to all their neighbors and told over and over again the wonderful experiences of that day. She could hardly wait for Monday.

On *Shem en Naseem* Karma wakened before daylight. She tiptoed downstairs and cut a slice of onion. She went back to the bedroom and held it under the noses of her mother and father to waken them. That was the way they began "Smell the Breezes" day. Then Karma put on her new dress. The family admired it once more. Then they all got ready quickly and started down the street. Habeeb carried a picnic breakfast, which the mother had prepared the evening before, in a large basket. Karma's mother carried the baby astride one shoulder. The mother said Karma had been a big help in preparing the picnic breakfast and taking care of the little brother.

Although it was barely dawn, many people were already out. Families and groups of relatives were walking along the streets toward the river. All were talking and laughing. Most were wearing bright new clothes. They called to friends they met. As they passed a number of homes where rich people lived, servants standing beside the gates invited passers-by to come in and enjoy the gardens. Some people went in to eat their breakfasts and were allowed to pick roses.

Karma's family went on to the public gardens near the river. Karma loved the flowering trees and the soft green grass. Most of all she enjoyed watching sailboats glide by on the river. The family sat on the grass and ate their breakfast of hard-boiled eggs, ripe olives, white cheese, bread, and bananas.

Family groups were wandering around the public gardens, and

Karma was glad when she saw Suad with her family. Suad's father came to ask Habeeb if they would like to take a boat ride on the Nile. A boatman was offering to take passengers for a few piasters. Habeeb agreed and Karma was happy all her family could go. This was the first time she rode on the river in a sailboat.

By the time they got off the boat they were all tired and ready to start home. As they went toward their house Karma said, "This has been the best holiday of my life, because I helped get ready for it."

—A STORY FROM EGYPT BY MARGARET M. MCCUTCHAN

# Hold April

Hold on to April; never let her pass!
   Another year before she comes again
To bring us wind as clean as polished glass
   And apple blossoms in soft, silver rain. . . .

Do not let April go but hold her tight,
Month of eternal beauty and delight.
          —LINES FROM *"Hold April"*
            BY JESSE STUART

# April Night and the Singing Winds

I choose this night and know the paths to take
Through sumacs, red oaks, winding like a snake.

Night voices call me back where I belong,
To rising winds that sing a red-brush song.

The sickle moon hangs low above the hills
And beams upon the splashing April rills. . . .

My blood runs wild but wilder is my mood;
I'm free to listen to the music flood!

Let wild winds sing across the April night
And dreamers ride the winds in gold starlight!

I'm glad to follow fox paths, shout and sing
I am alive on a night in April spring!
—LINES FROM *"April Night and the Singing Winds"*

BY JESSE STUART

# April on the Coast of Maine

April begins with May airs. The adder casts his skin and leaves it like a curl of spring sky on the hot ledge; and the farmer sloughs off his thick flannels. The south slopes of the hills scent the south winds with May flowers. The sun comes out hot. Brooks run like wildfire. Catkins shake out their gilt tassels on the poplar trees. Comes a freeze, and the loud little brooks fall quiet. It snows deep. The sun comes out strong. All the snow melts. The ducks are wild on many sudden waters.

The cosset lamb grows into a burden and is turned out of the kitchen to fend for himself where the green blades of grass are pricking through the world. It rains, and it clears. It rains, and it shines.

The feast of the season is alewives, for the fattest of the herring have returned and the land near all the brooks is frosted with their scales. The Abenaki fish steam in all the kitchens, and the rich aroma of it baking and roasting and frying and broiling and boiling and sousing in vinegar goes out over the whole house.

Frog spawns string miles of jet-and-crystal beads through the marsh pond. The small boy is up to his neck in watery business, and the new rubber boots come home full of water. In the swamps the tree

225

stumps bleed a honey that attracts the gilt flies. Now the farmer looks to his plow, his whiffletrees, and his axles; there is great mending of cart wheels; gear is made ready against the minute the frost is all out of the ground.

Suddenly, one clear twilight, under the first dewdrop star, the peepers begin, their silvery notes spread out thick as the stars are over the meadows. Ways grow foul, carts go hub-deep in yellow mud. A fortnight passes with no getting to town.

A wild gander goes over the waves with a taut neck stretched toward Labrador. The yellow dog sheds his hair, and he is a burden to the housekeeper. The crows meet in vast conclave at the ebb of the tide and gorge themselves on young crabs and broken clams the clam-diggers have left. Partridges grow fat on the birch buds.

The earliest bluets whiten the hill under the beeches, and the first dogtooth violets cover the valleys with leaves like spotted snakes. The robins come in from the South and begin pairing. The bluebirds fall like flakes of sky upon the red maples. The skunk cabbage unrolls scarlet in the swamp, and the bees come to pay their first call. The woodpecker fills all the woods and the world with his hollow knocking. There is much rubbing of noses and playing of tag among the rabbits. The children play tag late till the stars are hung on the birches.

Now the bay blossoms with white-and-green buoys, the new lobster boat is ready, and the man of the farm comes home laden with dark green dragons. The small boy stands by his father and heads out to sea; the spray from the bone in her mouth snows them over and over. The sea gulls have come down from inland, they follow the boat and the bait, they cry high for joy of the sea and spring. The girls are papering the playhouse. White herring are climbing the falls of the stream to lay their eggs in sweet water. There are dirty patches of snow in the sprucewoods still, but green grass is pricking the south-sloping side of ditches.

The woodchuck is full of tender sprouts, and he meditates an addition to his family and a new sitting-room. The hylas and frogs sing faster and faster, and the long evenings are like a thousand sleigh bells.

Taurus now is the sign, the little ram lambs leap up with stiff legs five feet into the sky, they jump over their mother and race six together the length of the meadow. The days are quicksilver, the evenings clear amber. Fresh food comes dripping from the flats and the fathoms. The small boy makes the small girl with the molasses-colored curls a willow whistle on the long way from school.

The bluebirds are back, the robins are back; the yellowhammers, the song sparrows come in with a rush at sunup; birds fill the woods with rolling bubbles of music.

The brush is taken away from the house, and new brush fires send up zigzagging stars. The big boy and his father get their dip nets and go through the dusk to the surging brook with a lantern. The small boy tags along. The arrows of smelts come up over the rocks, then men dip them out of the air and the pools, the small boy takes off his cap and fills it with live slivers of silver. They fry the fish by the water's edge, and eat them with scraps of salt pork in an ecstasy under an arch of stars.

Ponds break up now, and the trout rises to the slender green flies. The new baby smiles his first smile, and the whole family are proud to see it.

The girls make many paper baskets and hang them deep with pink, green, blue, and yellow curls of tissue, twisting it up into long curls like their own with a flick of the blade of scissors. The small boy does trailing clouds of tissue streamers to Molasses-Curls' house.

His heart pounds louder than the knocker on the door, he drops the May basket, gumdrops and all, and he runs for dear life.

It is a month of buds and little boys in love, and of great promises, for all its mud and snow, and life moves out of the house at last and under the good sun.

—FROM *"April"* IN *Coast Calendar*
BY ROBERT P. TRISTRAM COFFIN

# April Fools' Day

The first of April, some do say,
Is set apart for All Fools' Day;
But why the people call it so
Nor I, nor they themselves, do know.
But on this day are people sent
On purpose for pure merriment.

. . . In sending fools to get intelligence
One seeks hen's teeth in farthest part of the town;
Another pigeon's milk; a third a gown
From strolling cobbler's stall, left there by chance;
Thus lead the giddy tribe a merry dance.

And thus did *Poor Robin's Almanack* picture the first of April in England about 1760.

How did it all begin? No one knows. Some writings indicate it was observed in Europe at least three hundred years ago, and it is believed the celebration of All Fools' Day may have gone to England from France. When France adopted the Gregorian calendar in 1564, New Year's Day, a traditional time of gift giving, moved from March 25 to January 1. Jokers, however, continued to give mock gifts during the former New Year season, which may have extended from March 25 to April 1. Others suggest the observance of April Fool's Day may have originated as a Jesters' Day or Fools' Day in honor of those who by their actions and wit kept kings and noblemen amused.

—MILDRED CORELL LUCKHARDT

229

# Archie and the April Fools

"Ted," said Jimmy Brewster, coming into the living room rather suddenly. "I hate to mention it, but there's a giraffe in the backyard."

His brother roused himself from the study of a photograph, gave Jimmy a puzzled look, then glanced at the calendar. A peaceful smile dawned upon his face. The calendar unquestionably proclaimed the fact that it was April 1.

"Run away, my good man," said Ted. "I'm busy. You know, Jimmy, there's definitely a light leak in our camera. We've certainly got to get a new one, as soon as we have enough money."

"We're going to get a projector," Jimmy reminded him, "and, while I hate to mention it again, there is a giraffe in our backyard."

"I know, I know. And there's a baby hippopotamus in the kitchen sink, too, but don't bother me with that now. Just put April Fool's Day out of your mind." Ted sighed. "What kind of camera do you think we should get?"

"Projector," said Jimmy gazing thoughtfully out of the window. "I take it all back. There isn't a giraffe in the backyard."

Ted said: "That's better. You can't catch me on those old April Fool gags."

"He isn't in the backyard," said Jimmy, "because now he's in the sideyard."

Ted fixed his brother with a glittering eye. "Now look here, you poor cluck, enough's enough. Once is funny, but—" He broke off, his gaze drawn to the window by Jimmy's intent start, and made a noise like a drowning suction pump.

"You see?" said Jimmy reproachfully.

Ted saw. He rushed to the window and peered out wildly. Jimmy nodded in sympathy. He knew how Ted felt. But there was no getting away from it—the large spotted object in the Brewster peony bed was a giraffe.

"I hope," said Jimmy, with dignity, "that this will be a lesson to you to trust me. I was deeply hurt—"

"Stop babbling," Ted requested, recovering slightly. "What are we going to do about this—this monster?"

Jimmy gazed out at the giraffe, which had left the peony bed and was munching a convenient tree, its head out of sight and its long thin neck looking like a large spotted serpent.

"I read a book once," said Jimmy.

"This is no time to discuss your literary exploits," his brother told him fiercely. "Great howling buttercups! We've got to *do* something."

"This book," said Jimmy, undiscouraged, "said that giraffes can run faster than most horses."

"Yoicks! We've got to catch him. He probably belongs to the zoo."

"Maybe it would be better just to leave him alone," said Jimmy. "The book also said they kick with their hind legs, and, while naturally gentle, are capable of making a stout resistance."

Ted, who had been about to leave the house and organize a

giraffe hunt, stopped in his tracks. "Stout resistance, huh? Perhaps we'd better call the zoo first."

"You watch the giraffe, and I'll call 'em." Jimmy grabbed for the phone book. "Circle 2-1023. Hurry, operator . . . Hello, hello. Look this is Jimmy Brewster, out on the Pine Road. We've got a giraffe here . . . *A giraffe.* One of those things from Africa with long necks . . . I want your what? Your accounting department? I do *not* want your accounting department. I want—" He broke off suddenly. "Look, what number is this?" . . . Oh. Oh, I see. I'm sorry." He hung up, rather sadly. "That was the bank. They said I wanted their accounting department."

"Get going," Ted advised. "He's eating the lilac bush now."

"Circle 2-1023," Jimmy said again into the phone. "Ted, if you were a bank, would you refer a giraffe to your accounting department? . . . Hello. Is this the zoo? . . . Well, have you lost a giraffe? Yes. Yes? You have? . . . Well, it's here in our peony bed."

"Lilac," said Ted.

"Lilac bed," Jimmy corrected himself. "What do you want us to do?" There followed a brief, rather one-sided conversation, then Jimmy said, "Thank you. Yes, sure, we will."

He hung up.

"What'd they say?"

"It belongs to the zoo all right. They're sending men out with a truck, and we're to keep the giraffe here until they come." He paused. "Ted, there's a $25 reward for the thing. He said we'd get it, if we caught the giraffe."

"Zowie!" Ted shouted. "We can get that camera."

"Projector," said Jimmy automatically.

"Camera," said Ted. "All we have to do—" He stopped short. "Faster than a horse, huh? Suppose it runs away when it sees us?

Maybe it's scared of people." "Frankly," said Jimmy, "that would make it unanimous. I'm scared of it."

Ted waved his hand airily. "Don't be difficult. Look, you go and get the encyclopedia and see what it says about giraffes, while I watch the beast out the window."

Jimmy dashed off and returned with the required volume. Ted, who had been watching the giraffe anxiously, said: "One of the advantages of living in the country is there's plenty of giraffe food around. He's eating the ivy now. Mother and Dad won't be pleased."

"Well, if they were home," said Jimmy reasonably, "they could tell Archie so."

"Archie?"

"That's his name. The zoo man told me." He began to read. "The giraffe or camelopard—good night, is that what he is? A camelopard!"

"Go on," said Ted.

Jimmy went on. "Native of Africa—occurs generally in herds of from five to forty. Whoops! Not here, I hope. Feeds on leaves and small branches of trees. Yes, we'd guessed that. Seven vertebrae in neck. Hey! That all I've got. It hardly seems fair. Look at the length of his neck compared to mine."

If you don't get a move on," Ted warned him dangerously, "there won't be any Archie here to have a neck."

Jimmy read on hastily. "No vocal chords—well, anyway, he can't answer back then. Generally seeks safety in flight—that's not so good. Large, clear eyes—nice for Archie, but no use to us. Ah, here we are!"

"About time," said Ted bitterly.

"What I said about their kicking with their hind legs," said Jimmy, "is true. But it seems they only kick lions."

"What do you mean, they only kick lions?"

"Well, the lion is their natural enemy, so, when attacked by a lion, they kick it—naturally."

"Very sensible point of view," Ted approved heartily. "Well, you and I aren't lions, therefore Archie won't kick us. Elementary, my dear Watson. Let's go."

Jimmy looked unhappy.

"Twenty-five dollars reward," Ted reminded him, "means we can get that camera."

"Projector," said Jimmy.

"Camera," said Ted. "Come on."

His brother came.

They let themselves cautiously out the back door and, by creeping, managed to get within ten feet of their giraffe, before it noticed them. At that point, however, Jimmy fell over the garden hose and

into an empty pail, and, the clatter being considerable, Archie withdrew his narrow head from the treetop.

"Shush!" said Ted, fiercely.

Jimmy removed himself from the pail with as much dignity as possible. "I couldn't help it. Some silly idiot left that hose across the path."

"You did," said Ted. "Last night."

The giraffe was regarding them in a benign and lofty manner. "The man said to be awfully careful with him," Jimmy said. "He cost $3,500."

"That thing?" Ted regarded Archie with profound respect. "Well, I'll be hornswoggled! What's he got that I haven't got?"

"More neck," said Jimmy, "and spots with white edgings."

Ted treated this remark with the contempt it deserved. "This is going to be quite simple," he announced suddenly, in a competent

manner. "He's perfectly friendly." He stretched out one hand placatingly and began to advance, a step at a time. "Here, Archie, Archie. Nice Archie . . . Oops!"

Archie gave him one look, shied violently, wheeled, and departed around the corner of the house, his sloping body rolling in a ridiculous amble. "Now, look what you've done," said Jimmy. "There goes our projector."

"Camera," said Ted. "Come on. We've got to catch him."

They rushed around the house and stopped short.

"There he is!" Jimmy panted, pointing. "He's stopped. Hey! Ought he to do that?"

The giraffe had sighted a yellow crocus in the grass, and it had evidently roused in him a desire for dessert. Accordingly, he had spread his thin forelegs out at an impossible angle and was lowering his head earthwards, in a way that looked extremely perilous.

"He doesn't look safe to me," said Ted. "Besides, for all we know, crocuses aren't good for giraffes. Do they have crocuses in Africa?"

"I don't know," said Jimmy, "but I'll go and get the encyclopedia, while you figure out a way to—"

"Oh, no, you don't," Ted said firmly, grabbing his brother and hauling him back. "I've already figured out a way. How soon do they expect to get here from the zoo?"

"Dunno," Jimmy admitted regretfully. "It's quite a ways, and they may not find our place right off, although I gave 'em directions. Why?"

"If that giraffe leaves," said Ted, "our new camera leaves."

"Projector," said Jimmy.

Ted ignored him. "And the chances are that Archie isn't going to hang around just to oblige us. So *my* idea is to get him into our barn. It's got a good high roof, and—"

"May I ask just one simple little question?" said Jimmy. "*How* are you going to get him into the barn? You can't lead him, you know. He's all neck and legs. There's nothing to hang onto."

Ted said dramatically, "Look at his tail!"

Jimmy looked. It was a goodish tail, not beautiful, perhaps, but certainly utilitarian, with tuft on the end. It would be a most satisfactory tail to hang onto.

"Well?" said Ted.

"I can think of two objections," Jimmy said. "One is, do you think you can pull a giraffe around backwards? Because, if so, I'm going to leave the whole thing to you, and you can have the projector all to yourself. I have my life to live."

"It's going to be a camera," Ted said firmly, "and we don't pull him, you goof. We urge him forward gently. The tail is just for emergencies, in case he starts to run."

"Oh," said Jimmy. "Well, the other objection is the location of his tail."

"Well, naturally, but the usual place is so awfully near his heels." Jimmy looked mournful and quoted, " 'They kick with their hind legs and are capable of making a stout resistance.' "

"So what?" said Ted. "Archie won't attack anything but a lion. You read that yourself from the encyclopedia. We aren't lions, are we?" There was a short pause.

"I see what you mean," said Jimmy. "Are we men or are we lions?" There was another short pause. "Personally, I'm a mouse. You do it, Ted. You're more the executive type. I'll watch."

"You will not," Ted told him. "It's perfectly simple. I'll go in front and urge him on with some grass, and you go behind and hang onto his tail."

"Me?" Jimmy croaked. "Hang onto his tail?"

"Certainly. You just said I was the executive type, didn't you? Well, the executive type always leads. Come on, Jimmy."

Ted gave him a shove from behind, and Jimmy staggered mournfully toward Archie's tail, stared at it for a moment, took a deep breath, and grabbed.

Things after that happened very quickly. Archie's left hind leg kicked out at a fantastic angle and landed a powerful and accurate wallop. Jimmy described a parabola in the air, rolled over twice on the grass, got to his feet, and started running.

Ted joined him. Archie galloped in enthusiastic pursuit. His two would-be captors shot up into the branches of the nearest apple tree, and Archie came to a disappointed halt. Jimmy and Ted climbed upward as far as they could and came to rest near an abandoned bird's nest. They looked at each other.

"Kicks only lions," said Jimmy bitterly, "The executive type. Bah!"

"You read the book yourself," Ted accused and looked down thoughtfully at Archie's head, weaving around among the branches. The tree was not tall, and Archie was. After a moment, Ted broke off some juicy-looking leaves and handed them down to Archie, who accepted them courteously. Ted broke off some more.

Jimmy got the idea and began to help. "If we can only keep him here until the zoo men come—"

"I hope the tree lasts out," said Ted. "Sit down, Jimmy. You're rocking the boat."

"Thank you," said his brother with dignity. "I'm more comfortable standing up."

Ted said, "Oh," with polite sympathy, and Jimmy added: "In case you want to know, being kicked by an even-toed ungulate is the same as being kicked by anything else, only rougher."

"By a what?"

"An even-toed ungulate. That's what that thing down there is. And, personally, I wish he'd go off and ungulate somewhere else."

"Think of the camera," Ted urged.

"I am thinking," said Jimmy, "of the projector." He added broodingly: "So he wouldn't kick me, huh? He wouldn't kick me because I didn't have a mane. Phooey!" He then said, "Whoops!" and nearly fell out of the tree.

A large, purposeful-looking truck had just turned into the driveway.

"The zoo men!" Ted shouted. "The marines have landed. Jimmy, we're saved." He hesitated, and added: "I wish we weren't up here, though. It doesn't look so good. They might almost think Archie caught *us*."

"If they give that giraffe the reward," said Jimmy, "I shall blow a fuse." "Hey!" said a voice. A stout man in blue overalls was peering up at them, one arm wound affectionately around Archie's neck. "What you doing up there?"

Jimmy said, "We've caught the giraffe for you," and there was a hearty burst of laughter in reponse.

"Look who's caught who, will you?" said the stout man. "A nice, tame, little fellow like Archie, too!"

"Tame!" said Ted under his breath, and then addressed the stout man quite coolly. "We couldn't find much for him to eat, and we thought feeding him was the best way to keep him here." He paused impressively. "We're up in this tree, where we can get more leaves."

The stout man was silenced in his turn, and Jimmy and Ted descended with admirable dignity. "Well," the man admitted finally, "that was pretty smart. Yessir, that was real bright. We're much

obliged. I'll see you get that reward all right."

Indoors, Jimmy glared at the encyclopedia. "Only lions," he muttered.

"We can get our camera," Ted offered consolingly.

"*Projector!*" Jimmy howled.

"M'mmmm," said Ted, "I'll tell you what. We'll compromise. Next time we'll buy a projector. This time we'll buy a camera. Now run along and get some cookies, there's a pal. All that brain work has made me hungry." Jimmy gazed upon his brother in mingled awe and fury, said "Compromise!" in a strangled voice, then departed suddenly. He came back a moment later, both hands full of cookies and a strange glitter in his eyes.

"Ted," he said, "I hate to mention it. But there's a rhinoceros in the back yard."

Ted let out a wild scream and dashed into the kitchen. A moment later, Jimmy heard the back door slam. A gentle smile dawned on his face.

"Ah, well," he murmured, "we can't all be the executive type."

He looked affectionately at the calendar, which still proclaimed unmistakably that it was April Fool's Day, smiled again, and began to eat his cookies. He felt much better.

—B. J. CHUTE

# Surprise!

Easter was a joyous day. The weather was perfect. April Bright was a very happy girl. Flowers bloomed everywhere, and the first tulips opened. There was only one dark one, but it did look rich and beautiful among the others. April remembered that one day when she was unhappy because someone had remarked unkindly about her dark skin, her mother had said that the dark blossoms made a bouquet rich and beautiful. Mother had added, "You're my dark April. Dark April Bright. You're a Brownie too! Isn't that funny."

Today everyone was outdoors and dressed in his best. April wore the dress and the hat Mamma had made from April's design. She felt cool and very quiet inside. Mrs. Bright had a new veil and flowers on last year's hat, and even April's brother Tom was spruced up in a new suit, though Father said he couldn't very well afford it so soon after paying taxes.

"We haven't much choice in the matter," said Mamma when Mr. Bright finally took Tom to buy it. "He has grown so that his arms stick out of his sleeves like pipestems, and his trousers are threadbare."

So Tom came down the stairs Easter morning, clattering his

242

drumsticks in a new pattern on each step edge, and ending with a flourish to show how elegant he was in his new clothes.

The church was crowded. It was wonderful to hear the joyous Easter music after the sad service on Friday, and to see the flowers that were banked about the pulpit. April's sister Chris, who was a nurse, came home for a while in the afternoon, and it was a very happy day.

School began again on Tuesday, and with it came rain. Cherry blossoms fell like snowflakes but left behind them on the branches the little green knobs that would swell into red cherries.

"I guess this is the cherry rain," Mamma said, "and it may last for several days."

But by Thursday, when it was time for Brownie meeting, the sky was clear again. The leaves had grown so fast that the street looked like summer, but the air was cold. When April woke in the morning she heard the robins as usual, a crow squawking overhead, and then she heard a new sound. First she thought it was a cardinal, then a wren; next she thought it was only the robin, after all, but when the song changed again and again, she was sure it was a new bird to add to her list. She jumped out of bed and ran to the window to see if she could locate the sound. Mamma came into the room to wake her and found her up.

"Up already?" she said in surprise. But April cautioned her to be quiet and come to the window.

"It's a new bird," she whispered. "It's up there in the maple, but I can't find it. Can you, Mamma?"

Mamma pointed to the dead branch over the shed. "There he is," she whispered back. "It's a catbird. But he isn't new. He's been building his nest at the back of the garden for several years. You just weren't seeing birds before, that's all. See how neat and tidy he is? He's a kind of mocking bird. Hear that? He's making believe he's a cardinal now."

"Do you mean he's been coming here right along and I never heard him before?" April asked wonderingly.

"Yes, of course," Mamma answered. "Just as the tulip tree has stood at the back of the garden in the next yard ever since long before we came here. Yet you said you had never seen a tulip tree till your Brownie Scouts took that walk and the Girl Scout nature counselor, Flicker, showed you those along Wissahickon Creek. We get used to going about with unseeing eyes and unhearing ears. It is only when something catches our interest that we really *see* it and know about it."

April nodded. It was so. Just knowing that the maple tree in the yard was a *silver* maple made her see it. She had never noticed it before and could hardly have told that there was a tree in the backyard!

Flicker came to the meeting that afternoon to talk over the walk the Brownies had taken along the Wissahickon and to see who had the longest list of birds and trees.

"Brownies don't work for badges," she had said, "but if you begin to know the trees and the creatures of the woods and to recognize the birds, you will be that much more ready to be real Girl Scouts."

April was nearly old enough now to "fly up" to Scouts. She would be ten in just a week. She had learned to know ten trees and twelve birds. How she hoped her list would be longest!

While Mrs. Cole, the leader, kept the girls busy cleaning out ink bottles to begin ink-bottle gardens for Mother's Day presents, Flicker took each girl in turn into the other room to question her about what she had learned.

"There is a surprise for the girl who has the longest list of birds and of trees. After we find out *who* it is, I will tell you *what* it is," Flicker promised.

Each girl, as she came back after the questioning, just giggled, or pursed her lips, or put her tongue in her cheek, according to her nature, but none of them spoke. April knew that Sophie had almost as many trees as she did, but she was pretty sure that her list of birds was not as long. When Sophie came dancing back into the room with a wide smile and a look that said, "I know something I won't tell," April was sure her chance for the surprise was gone.

Finally her turn came. She told Flicker about the mourning dove she had seen and how much smaller it is than the pigeon; and about the low mourning sound it makes and how if you see one you nearly always see another one nearby. She told about the blue jay and his thieving habits and how he even dug up the nuts the squirrels buried in the back yard. She could recognize his harsh cry and told Flicker how she had read that sometimes he does good deeds by burying seeds that grow into trees. She told about the cardinal, the crow, and the brown thrasher with his speckled breast; the song sparrow that looks so plain and mouse-colored but sings so sweetly. Last of all, she told about the catbird she had heard and seen that very morning; how he trilled and whistled, chirped and twittered; how he mewed like a cat and laughed like a jay.

After that came the list of trees. Besides those she had learned to know in the neighborhood and in the little park, there were the ones she had learned on the walk, and Mamma had told her to look for the copper beech and the horse chestnut growing in gardens down on Greene Street.

When Flicker came in to tell them who was to have the surprise, she said, "I would like to tell you that you have all won, you have done so well. But this time it must be just one of you, and I know you will be happy that it is someone who deserves it." The girls began to clap their hands and chatter so loud that Mrs. Cole held up her hand for quiet.

Flicker went on: "This someone is almost ready to fly up, for she will be ten in just a week." April twisted her hands in a tight clasp. She would be ten in a week! "I have been careful to see which of you has the most points to her credit," Flicker continued, "and I find it is April Bright. So April is the one to have the surprise this time." Flicker looked at April's shining face as she went on:

"It is to be a supper party to be given at Deep Meadow Farm. There is to be just one Brownie from each of eight different troops and the leader from that troop. So Mrs. Cole gets a surprise too! And—it falls on April's birthday!" April's face felt warm and glowing, but the dryness in her throat wouldn't let her say how happy she was, so she only grinned and showed two rows of beautiful white teeth.

—FROM *Bright April* BY MARGUERITE DE ANGELI

# When Daffodils Begin to Peer

When daffodils begin to peer,
    With heigh! the doxy over the dale,
Why, then comes in the sweet o' the year;
    For the red blood reigns in the winter's pale.
        —WILLIAM SHAKESPEARE


# An April Day

On such a day as this I think,
    On such a day as this,
When earth and sky and nature's whole
    Are clad in April's bliss;
And balmy zephyrs gently waft
    Upon your cheek a kiss;
Sufficient is it just to live
    On such a day as this.
        —JOSEPH S. COTTER, JR.

# Rain Music

On the dusty earth-drum
  Beats the falling rain;
Now a whispered murmur,
  Now a louder strain.

Slender, silvery drumsticks,
  On an ancient drum,
Beat the mellow music
  Bidding life to come.

Chords of earth awakened,
  Notes of greening spring,
Rise and fall triumphant
  Over every thing.

Slender, silvery drumsticks
  Beat the long tattoo—
God, the Great Musician,
  Calling life anew.

—JOSEPH S. COTTER, JR.

*When the West was being settled, many homesteaders staked claims to land in springtime and built rough shelters where their families could live. The Ingalls family were homesteaders and their adventures are favorite stories for thousands of readers. When Pa started the beginnings of a homestead on his new claim by the shores of Silver Lake in Dakota territory, Laura, oldest of the four girls, was nearly thirteen and a great help to Pa and Ma. Laura generally took very good care of Grace, the baby. Then, suddenly, one day when they were planting trees around the cabin, Grace disappeared. Each one thought the other was watching her. Pa and Ma started at once toward the Big Slough. Laura stood for a moment trembling with fear and then started running across the prairie. Laura tells in her own words what happened that day in the story which follows. It is a part of the chapter, "Where Violets Grow," from the book BY THE SHORES OF SILVER LAKE.*

# Where Violets Grow

Laura was running straight toward the south. Grass whipped soft against her bare feet. Butterflies fluttered over the flowers. There wasn't a bush nor a weed that Grace could be hidden behind. There was nothing, nothing but grass and flowers swaying in the sunshine.

If she were little and playing all by herself, Laura thought, she wouldn't go into the dark Big Slough, she wouldn't go into the

249

mud and the tall grass. Oh, Grace, why didn't I watch you? she thought. Sweet pretty little helpless sister—"Grace! Grace!" she screamed. Her breath caught and hurt in her side.

She ran on and on. Grace must have gone this way. Maybe she chased a butterfly. She didn't go into Big Slough! She didn't climb the hill, she wasn't there. Oh, baby sister, I couldn't see you anywhere east or south on this hateful prairie. "Grace!"

The horrible, sunny prairie was so large. No lost baby could ever be found on it. Ma's calling and Pa's shouts came from Big Slough. They were thin cries, lost in the wind, lost on the enormous bigness of the prairie.

Laura's breathing hurt her sides under the ribs. Her chest was smothering and her eyes were dizzy. She ran up a low slope. Nothing, nothing, not a spot of shadow was anywhere on the level prairie all around her. She ran on, and suddenly the ground dropped before her. She almost fell down a steep bank.

There was Grace. There, in a great pool of blue, sat Grace. The sun shone on her golden hair blowing in the wind. She looked up at Laura with big eyes as blue as violets. Her hands were full of violets. She held them up to Laura and said, "Sweet! Sweet!"

Laura sank down and took Grace in her arms. She held Grace carefully and panted for breath. Grace leaned over her arm to reach more violets. They were surrounded by masses of violets blossoming above low-spreading leaves. Violets covered the flat bottom of a large, round hollow. All around this lake of violets, grassy banks rose almost straight up to the prairie-level. There in the round, low place the wind hardly disturbed the fragrance of the violets. The sun was warm there, the sky was overhead, the green walls curved all around, and butterflies fluttered over the crowding violet faces.

Laura stood up and lifted Grace to her feet. She took the violets that Grace gave her, and clasped her hand. "Come, Grace," she said. "We must go home."

She gave one look around the little hollow while she helped Grace climb the bank.

Grace walked so slowly that for a little while Laura carried her. Then she let her walk, for Grace was nearly three years old, and heavy. Then she lifted her again. So, carrying Grace and helping her walk, Laura brought her to the shanty and gave her to Mary.

Then she ran toward the Big Slough, calling as she ran. "Pa! Ma! She's here!" She kept on calling until Pa heard her and shouted to Ma, far in the tall grass. Slowly, together, they fought their way out of Big Slough and slowly came up to the shanty, draggled and muddy and very tired and thankful.

"Where did you find her, Laura?" Ma asked, taking Grace in her arms and sinking into her chair.

"In a—" Laura hesitated, and said, "Pa, could it really be a fairy ring? It is perfectly round. The bottom is perfectly flat. The bank around it is the same height all the way. You can't see a sign of that place till you stand on the bank. It is very large, and the whole bottom of it is covered solidly thick with violets. A place like that couldn't just happen, Pa. Something made it."

"You're too old to be believing in fairies, Laura," Ma said gently. "Charles, you must not encourage such fancies."

"But it isn't—it isn't like a real place, truly," Laura protested. "And smell how sweet the violets are. They aren't like ordinary violets."

"They do make the whole house sweet," Ma admitted. "But they are real violets and there are no fairies."

"You are right, Laura; human hands didn't make that place," Pa said. "But your fairies were big, ugly brutes, with horns on their heads and humps on their backs. That place is an old buffalo wallow. You know buffaloes are wild cattle. They paw up the ground and wallow in the dust, just as cattle do.

"For ages the buffalo herds had these wallowing places. They pawed up the ground and the wind blew the dust away. Then another herd came along and pawed up more dust in the same place. They went always to the same place, and—"

"Why did they, Pa?" Laura asked.

"I don't know," Pa said. "Maybe because the ground was mellowed there. Now the buffalo are gone, and grass grows over their wallows. Grass and violets."

—LAURA INGALLS WILDER

# The Flower-Fed Buffaloes

The flower-fed buffaloes of the spring
In the days of long ago,
Ranged where the locomotives sing
And the prairie flowers lie low;
The tossing, blooming, perfumed grass
Is swept away by wheat,
Wheels and wheels and wheels spin by
In the spring that still is sweet.
But the flower-fed buffaloes of the spring
Left us long ago.
They gore no more, they bellow no more,
They trundle around the hills no more:—
With the Blackfeet lying low,
With the Pawnees lying low.

—VACHEL LINDSAY

# Song: On a May Morning

Now the bright morning-star, day's harbinger,
Comes dancing from the east, and leads with her
The flowery May, who from her green lap throws
The yellow cowslip and the pale primrose.
Hail, bounteous May, that dost inspire
Mirth and youth and warm desire!
Woods and groves are of thy dressing,
Hill and dale doth boast thy blessing.
Thus we salute thee with our early song,
And welcome thee, and wish thee long.

—JOHN MILTON

# May Day—May 1

Perhaps May Day was celebrated long, long ago in some European lands where Druid priests led the people to worship trees and to hold ceremonies honoring the god Bel, or Baal. Since Bel was an ancient oriental god, some people who study history have suggested that various Beltane (or Bealtine) customs that were celebrated for many years in Scotland and Ireland, might have begun in ancient times in Asia. Beltane fires were lit in many places in Scotland and Ireland as part of the May festival, and were believed to scare away witches, protect cattle from disease, and bring spring warmth and sunshine more quickly.

Romans were among the ancient peoples who held a springtime festival to honor Flora, the goddess of flowers. Her statue was crowned with a wreath of flowers, and children wound ropes of flowers around the columns of her temple. Perhaps in many other parts of the world then children were making daisy chains and other floral chains in celebration of springtime, even as they do today.

In Floralia, the old Roman festival held in honor of Flora, goddess of flowers, even slaves were allowed to do whatever they wished so long as they returned home by night. Through the streets merrymakers raced and danced and sang and played tricks on each other. Sometimes the revelry became riotous, and sensible Romans kept their children indoors and did whatever they could to bring the revellers under control.

Festivals of spring flowers and trees have been held for centuries in many countries; and on May Day or some similar day groups of people have gone happily into the fields and woods to bring back flowers and branches of trees. From ancient times trees were believed to hold the power of new life. In England, where long ago Druids had held trees to be sacred, May trees or Maypoles were brought back to towns and villages, and people danced about them on May Day.

After a while, when people no longer worshiped trees as the bringers of new life, they still held some of the old superstitions about the Maypole and about the sprigs of green brought from the woods. In time May Day became one of the merriest days of the year. In parts of England young people who had been out "maying" in the woods and fields since midnight, returned in the morning with arms laden with blossoms and greens. They especially were fond of branches of rosy-pink hawthorn blossoms, which were called branches of "the may." Then they would go through the village, giving out flowers and singing an old May carol, some of which is:

> We've been rambling all of the night,
> And some time of this day,
> And now returning back again
> We bring you a branch of May.
> A branch of May we bring you here,
> And at your door we stand
> 'Tis only a sprout, but well budded out
> By the work of our Lord's hand.

Then, after doors had been decorated and the May really had been brought into the homes, there might be a gay procession with people in all sorts of costumes. A lively group dressed as Robin Hood and his merry men blew horns to announce the coming of the Queen of the May. She rode in a flower-trimmed cart and was crowned on the village green while people strewed flowers and cheered. Jesters rode around on hobby horses and played jokes. Often a chimney sweep, known as "Jack-in-the-Green" was borne along, hidden in a bower of leaves. Whenever he peeped out, people laughed; and when he suddenly sprang from beneath the leaves, the crowd cheered. The day was filled with pranks and games and singing and feasting and dancing around the big Maypole.

Now boys and girls all over the United States and in many countries sing and dance around the Maypole during May. And on May Day for centuries throughout the world people have given their friends gifts of flowers, either in bouquets or garlands, or in May baskets or leis, as in Hawaii. The first Christmas card prepared by UNICEF showed children of many lands joining hands and dancing around a Maypole.

—MILDRED CORELL LUCKHARDT

# May Day Is Lei Day in Hawaii

May Day in Hawaii is a time for giving garlands of fragrant plumeria, crisp orchids, delicate pikake, and spicy ginger. And it is a time for parades and pageants commemorating Hawaiian royalty and native warriors. School children and their parents pick their gardens bare of flowers to string into leis for the celebration.

The idea of setting aside a special day for paying tribute to the lei and the aloha spirit which it expresses was suggested by the late poet, Don Blanding, in 1928. A local newspaperwoman, Grace Tower Warren, was credited with giving him the slogan, "May Day Is Lei Day in Hawaii."

The first such celebration was held in the lobby of a downtown bank and was so popular that every available space in the bank was filled with flowers. Streets surrounding the building had to be blocked off to prevent traffic jams.

The May Day-Lei Day celebration soon outgrew the bank lobby and in later years was moved to the city hall and finally to the Waikiki Shell. Today there are lei contests with entries from all over the state. Of course there is a Lei Day queen and lei pole dances. It is a very special day, but some Hawaiians recall the past when

every day was lei day. "Leis used to be part of everyday attire. Going without a lei in the morning was like forgetting to comb your hair."

The lei was brought to the Hawaiian islands long, long ago by Polynesians who braved stormy seas to move from the Pacific islands to Hawaii. Leis were used originally by the Polynesian pioneers to appease angry gods and ward off evil spirits. But in Hawaii the newly arrived settlers soon realized they were freed from the troubles of the islands of their birth. Leis became a symbol of friendliness and have remained so for thousands of years.

The maile lei is probably the oldest of the Hawaiian leis. It was picked by tribes in the forests surrounding their villages. Hawaiian maile is similar to the myrtle that was awarded to Olympic winners in ancient Greece. The flower lei is believed to have originated in Southeast Asia where jasmine or pikake flowers were used in ancient times. The orange, feathery llima lei also is believed to have Asiatic origins. The old tradition of reserving the llima lei for the Hawaiian ruling classes may have derived from the fact that yellow is a symbol of learning and religion in India and a symbol of royalty in China.

Nearly everywhere May Day brings beauty and pleasure. In Hawaii it has the added enchantment of Lei Day.

—ADAPTED FROM AN ARTICLE WRITTEN BY DENBY FAWCETT

# May Day for Neighbors

I glared at Carmelita as we rode in opposite corners of our apartment house elevator up to the fifth floor. I hurried from it toward our apartment, but I could hear her steps clomping slowly the other way toward where she lived with her aunt and uncle. Why did she have to move so close to us from Brazil last month? And be in my class in school? I was furious with what she had done to me today!

My mother was cooking supper when I reached our kitchen. She smiled and patted my arm, asking "Did you have a happy day, dear?" But I brushed her hand aside and went into my bedroom and slammed the door. My little brother and sister who had been putting together puzzles on the kitchen table cried, "What's the matter with Rosalyn, Mommy?"

My older sister came to get a sweater from our bedroom and asked, "What's wrong?" But I snapped, "Go away! Let me alone!" And when Mother came to find out what troubled me I answered crossly, "Nothing!" and shut the door in her face.

Just then Father came home from work. He is a postman. He usually speaks quietly, but we children know he expects us to listen

262

and obey. "Rosalyn Harrison!" he called. When he thinks we need to pay special attention he says our full names. "You are acting rude. Come here and tell us what is wrong. Perhaps we can help."

He seated me at the kitchen table. The whole family sat around and listened while I blurted out my angry story about Carmelita. "Ever since she's come here from Brazil she's been a troublemaker. The kids can't stand her, and she hates us. She's been mean to everyone just because two weeks ago on April Fool Day Sylvia Liebowitz and Agnes O'Connor wore very full skirts the way Carmelita does, and spoke with her accent. It was only an April Fool joke."

"But it wasn't being nice to her," my little brother said. "Did they play April Fool jokes where she came from?"

I exclaimed, "How should I know? She should get to know our customs instead of getting mad at us. Why, the day after April Fool, she pushed ahead of Agnes on the cafeteria line and knocked her tray so that tomato soup spilled on Agnes' new yellow dress."

"What did Agnes do?" asked my little sister.

"She called Carmelita a stupid foreigner who couldn't speak English right and didn't even have any manners. But Carmelita only said, " 'Hah! You made fun of me on your April Fool Day. Wait 'til you see what I'll do to some of you.' "

I stopped short. I couldn't let the little ones know that Carmelita had threatened to spoil the Maypole we were planning for the neighborhood younger children on May Day. Carmelita had said that in some places people fought for their rights on May Day, and she was going to fight us then.

Although my family was waiting for me to finish telling what Carmelita had threatened to do, I quickly said, "She and Sylvia Liebowitz are both smart in math. They sit near each other. Yesterday when they were handing in math papers, Sylvia's fell on the

floor and Carmelita stepped on it and ground it with her foot. So Sylvia had to do it over again."

"What did the teacher say?" My little brother wanted to know.

"He didn't see what happened. But when Sylvia complained, Carmelita shrugged her shoulders and asked, "How could my foot reach that far?" Some teachers find her hard to get along with. At first she acted dumb, but lately she's rude."

"What happened today?" Mother asked.

I could hardly keep tears back as I told. "Today in art class I had just finished making a little ceramics bluebird and was holding it and telling Maria Rodriguez that I was going to give it to you, Mother, for Mother's Day, because you love birds and flowers. Along came Carmelita, banged into me, and knocked the bird to the floor."

My family gasped when I cried, "It smashed to bits! When I accused Carmelita of doing it, she acted very surprised. She said, 'Give your mother the pieces. She'll think they're beautiful because you're such a goody-girl whose mamma dresses her like a little lady.'"

Mother put her arm around me. "I know the bird was beautiful because you made it with love, remembering how very much I do like birds and flowers. But why do you think Carmelita acts so disagreeable?"

My big brother suggested that maybe Carmelita was jealous because we are a happy family and our parents take good care of us, while Carmelita's aunt and uncle are away from home all day. He added, "She may have more family in Brazil and misses them."

My little sister had an idea. "Maybe Carmelita never lived in a big, crowded city before. Maybe now that spring is here she misses flowers and trees and gardens."

I had to admit that made sense. Once I had seen a picture

Carmelita had painted of a garden full of flowers, with a girl in a full, red skirt bending over to smell them.

My older brother spoke again, very seriously. He always was figuring out why people did unfriendly or violent things. "You know, too, she may feel different from the rest of you because she's in a strange place where nobody else speaks Portuguese and she always has to keep learning more English, which is a strange language to her."

I nodded. "It could be a reason. But in our school we're from many places and races. Our ancestors came from Africa, and so did those of many of our friends; but we don't all think or speak exactly alike. We have many other friends, too—like Sylvia, who's Jewish; and Agnes, who's Irish; and Maria, who's Puerto Rican; and Susie, whose family are Chinese; and Lola, whose father is a Mohawk Indian. And we all love Mrs. Schultz, who still speaks with a German accent, and the Fiolas, whose grandfather speaks only Italian. They're all in our neighborhood, and we get along. But what kind of neighbor is Carmelita?"

My older sister said in her soft voice, "Carmelita has come alone into a strange situation. Even though she's carrying a chip on her shoulder, she probably wants to be friendly and doesn't know how. So she's trying to get attention the wrong way. You know that in our urban renewal housing project there are some unfriendly people who cause trouble; but Carmelita ought to be helped to see that there are many good neighbors here and that she has a place among them. I think she really needs friends."

I didn't say a word. How could a person be a good neighbor to anyone like Carmelita, or help her be a part of a community? I didn't know how I ever could be her friend. While I thought about it my mother began to tell something she learned from her grandmother when she was nine and was angry at a girl named Daisy, who lived near their farm in Virginia.

"One spring afternoon Grandmother and I were sitting under an apple tree that was in full bloom. The air was filled with the fragrance of blossoms and the singing of birds; but I was too angry about Daisy to enjoy the lovely day. Grandmother took some twigs and made a stick figure of me and one of Daisy. She placed us several feet apart on the ground. Then, with a stick, she drew a circle around me that kept Daisy out. She asked me, 'Rose, do you want to shut Daisy out alone? Or are your mind and your heart big enough to do this, wisely and kindly?' Grandmother erased the narrow circle with her foot and drew one wide enough to bring Daisy and me into one circle."

My big sister's eyes were shining. "Mother, I like that. There's a poem that says the same thing. It ends 'But love and I had the wit to win; We drew a circle that took him in.' "

We all understood what the two kinds of circles meant, and my big brother said, "It doesn't mean you have to be buddy-pals with everybody, but you must not be self-centered and narrow-minded. You have to have goodwill even for people who are hard to get along with. Who knows, you might become friends? At least you can be a good neighbor."

The clock struck six o'clock, and Mother jumped up. "Oh! We're a little late. Rosalyn, please set the table while I make the dumplings for the stew. The rest of you start your homework or practicing and get washed for supper in twenty minutes. Someone get Daddy's slippers so he can rest in the living room." She looked at my father proudly, saying, "Jesse, you must be very tired because you do so much walking all day. But I know you're one of the best postmen we have, and you're always so kind."

As my father left the kitchen he said in his quiet way, "Rosalyn, after the little ones are in bed, let us talk about what is best to do. I'm sorry your gift for Mother was broken."

While Mother made dumplings, I set the table and brought one of her geraniums from the window sill for a centerpiece on the table. She always had plants growing by the windows. "Mommy," I asked, "was it hard to leave the Virginia farm and come to New York when you were a big girl?"

"Very hard," she answered. "I missed the trees and flowers and walks by the brook. The city seemed so big and strange. Sometimes I was terribly lonely and homesick for my family and childhood friends." Then she smiled "But in a few years I met a fine young man, whom I married. And your father and I have a good life together; and we are a happy family together."

"We are!" I hugged her, sorry that I had been cross when I came home from school.

"Did you realize, Rosalyn, that even though all the changes in my life from the country to the city were hard to take, Daddy, also, had changes that were hard to take even though he still lives a few blocks from where he grew up here in the Bronx?"

"How's that?" I asked, placing the napkins at each place.

"Well, when Daddy was a boy, this whole area had little houses with small gardens back of them. Where this housing project now rises twelve stories high was an empty lot where Daddy and his friends played baseball. In the little garden at Daddy's home his mother raised roses and sometimes sold a few for parties; or she sent them to neighbors who were sick. And Daddy and his brothers kept pet rabbits in their backyard. Now all those houses have been torn down, and all the neighbors had to move, and a big highway goes through where their neighborhood was."

"Humh!" was all I said as I finished setting the table and pouring out the milk. I was thinking that all over our country and even in the rest of the world, many old neighborhoods were changing and people were moving into strange situations and didn't know their new neighbors. How did people help form a pleasant neighborhood? Mrs. Schultz, even though she was lame with arthritis, was a good neighbor, especially when she took care of the Rodriguez children when their mother was sick. Susie and her Chinese parents never said anything but what was kind about anyone, even though the people upstairs over them were very noisy. I thought of different people in our housing project who were helping this to become a pleasant new neighborhood, even though many must be homesick for their old neighborhoods. And my parents certainly did all they could to be good neighbors, without ever interfering in anyone's lives.

Soon our family was seated at the supper table, eating the delicious stew and dumplings. Mother told us more about her childhood on a Virginia farm. "On the first day of May, we had fun hanging May baskets on neighbors' doors. The afternoon before, a bunch of us children went into the woods to pick wild flowers. After we brought them home, we made little bunches, tying the stems with long grass or a string and kept them in water overnight. That evening we were busy making little paper baskets with handles to slip over doorknobs. Very early next morning we put our little bouquets in the baskets and ran quietly across the fields to hang our May baskets on friends' doors. Then we dashed away, trying not to be seen."

Mother looked thoughtful. "I always made specially pretty May baskets for my mother and father and grandmother. And after Grandmother had drawn the circles, I made a May basket for Daisy."

My little sister clapped her hands. "And, then, Mommy, you and Daisy were wonderful friends right away."

Mother said slowly, "I wouldn't say we were wonderful friends right away. Friendship usually doesn't grow that quickly. But I got the mean feelings out of my heart about Daisy, and I honestly tried to be kind and friendly and not shut her out of things. Little by little, we did become friendlier and very much happier."

Right then, I decided to make a May basket for Mother that year. Maybe one for Mrs. Schultz, too, would be a good idea. Maybe one for the Rodriguez family, who still missed the flowers of Puerto Rico. I didn't see how a May basket would do any good for Carmelita. No use even thinking of giving her one, for she'd probably throw it on the floor and stamp on it. Her idea of May Day was to cause trouble, and she really had threatened to spoil the Maypole dance for the little ones. We'd have to organize guards all around and chase her away if she started trouble. But, wasn't it too bad she wanted to ruin the fun? We just wouldn't let her.

While I was doing my homework on the kitchen table and Mother was putting the little ones to bed, the May baskets kept dancing through my head. But I couldn't go out in the fields and pick flowers for them. How could I earn money to buy flowers? Besides, we girls were all trying to make money to buy the material for the streamers for the Maypole. Fortunately, the man who owned the hardware store where my big brother worked in the afternoons was lending us a pole. Then I thought of Mr. Fiola. Perhaps I could work in his little flower shop for an hour each afternoon. Maybe, he'd pay me with flowers for the May baskets.

Mother always went down the hall for a few minutes each evening to see if she could do anything for Mrs. Schultz. She went tonight just before it was time for me to go to bed. So I went quickly into the living room and told Daddy about my plan and asked if it was alright with him. He was pleased about the May baskets and said Mr. Fiola would be a good person to work for. Also, I probably would learn a lot more about flowers and how to take care of them.

When I explained about needing to earn money for Maypole streamers and pretty paper for the May baskets, Daddy said, "I'll pay you seventy-five cents a week if you cook us a good dinner one night each week and do all the preparing and clearing up. This will give Mother a little rest." I was happy, for I could earn a dollar and a half before May Day. I promised Daddy that I'd cook the best meals I could, and kissed him "good-night."

"Just a minute, Rosalyn," he said, drawing me down on a footstool beside him. "You know I'm sorry for you about Carmelita, and I'm sorry for her because she acts that way. What do you plan to do for her? How will you become her neighbor?"

Ugh! Carmelita again! I'd almost forgotten about her in planning for May baskets. "Daddy, I don't know that I can do anything for Carmelita. I'm only one person. I wouldn't know where to begin."

"Rosalyn Harrison, you have told me that you hope to be a doctor when you grow up. Is that true?"

"I certainly do want to be a doctor, and I'm working hard in school to learn all I can. I know it will take years of hard work and whatever money we can make and save for it. But in the end I'll be a doctor."

Daddy patted my hand. "We'll help you all we can. But remember, being a doctor is not the end of hard work but the beginning of more work and responsibility. What do you think a doctor must do first if he wants to cure a person?"

I thought a while, then I realized that first he must find out what really is wrong with a person and try to discover what makes that person sick. When I said this, my father replied, "Why don't you do that in a gentle way for Carmelita? Without showing off you could try being happiness doctor for our neighborhood."

As I went to the bedroom my sisters and I shared, I thought of all the things my family had said might be reasons for Carmelita's acting as she did. Yet, how could I be a good neighbor to her? Once when I had asked her not to throw chewing-gum papers and such stuff in the grass near the house, she got a newspaper from the trash basket and tore it and threw it around. I wondered if I had been kind or fault-finding to her.

I got ready for bed quietly without turning on our bedroom light, because my little sister was asleep in her bed. I could hear my big brother and James O'Connor laughing over their checkers game in the kitchen while my big sister made fudge. It smelled good. Soon my parents and the boys would be eating some, and there would be plenty saved for me and the little ones for tomorrow. It was a comfortable feeling to be getting ready for bed, with all the family home happy and safe.

Before I settled down I looked outside at the big yard between the four tall apartment houses in our project. That was the place where we would put up the Maypole for the children to dance around. As I looked down into the yard I could see a girl, all alone, kicking a tin can. She kicked it around and around, with no special place to go. Her wide skirt flared out in the breeze, and even before she came under a light, I knew it was Carmelita. All alone! Just kicking around! I looked across and saw no lights from her apartment. Wasn't anyone home? Didn't anyone tell her when to go to bed and then come in later to kiss her good-night as my mother did?

That very moment I made up my mind I would make Carmelita a May basket, too. She might destroy it; or she might laugh at me and think I was babyish to make May baskets. But I'd make her one, anyway.

Next morning in school I told the girls what my family had said

about why Carmelita acted so disagreeable, and they agreed that she might be lonely. They decided to try to be pleasant to her, although they doubted that she would be pleasant to them. Then I told them about the May baskets I was going to make. At first Sylvia thought it was kid stuff; but soon they all thought it would be fun to do for neighbors near them. They began to plan how they would get flowers, or else they might even make paper flowers because Maria's mother would show them how. I never told them I would give a basket to Carmelita because I was afraid they'd think I was foolish.

During the next two weeks we were all so busy planning for the Maypole and making paper baskets and earning money for flowers and things that we didn't think much about Carmelita. Really we didn't see much of her, but when any of us did we were polite and tried to act friendly. One day Sylvia even picked up Carmelita's math paper when it dropped on the floor. Carmelita looked very surprised.

There was lots of work in the florist shop—sweeping floors, washing the glass cases, watering plants, answering the phone, even helping wait on customers. One day when I was at the counter I saw Carmelita gazing at a bouquet of yellow daisies in the window. She looked at them as if they were the most beautiful flowers in the world; then she walked away alone, as usual. Perhaps she had had flowers like that in Brazil. So that afternoon I added "yellow daisies for Carmelita" to the list of flowers I hoped to earn for the May baskets. One rose with some ferns would go in Daddy's basket, because he often talked of the roses his mother raised when he was a boy. Mother would get a few violets because she loved going into the woods for violets when she was a girl; and I might add small pink snapdragons.

Since I wanted the baskets to be a surprise I got the flowers ready in Mrs. Schultz's apartment on May Day eve and wrote each person's name on the right basket. My big brother's held one bachelor button with some greens; my big sister's, some small daffodils. The little ones each had a mixture of bright flowers. Mrs. Schultz would be surprised because she didn't know there was a basket for her. I could hardly wait for morning.

You should have heard the children squeal with joy when they opened our door after I had knocked and run away. All our family stood in the doorway holding their May baskets and smiling. My little brother came racing down the hall carrying his when I was trying to run away after ringing Carmelita's bell. First she saw the May basket on the door knob and picked it up as if she were holding a whole beautiful flower garden in her hands. She could hardly believe it. At that moment my brother bumped into me and squawked and dropped his May basket. Carmelita saw us, as we scrambled around picking up his flowers.

Carrying her basket carefully, she came to help us. I could tell she didn't know what to say. Words wouldn't come. She just smiled and said "Thank you, Rosalyn," in sort of a whisper.

We had tests in school that day, so none of us had a chance to get together. Our minds were on the tests; but we, also, were eager to get home and start the Maypole dance for the little children in our housing project. Somehow, I could tell that ever since we had stopped making fun of Carmelita she had given up the idea of fighting us on May Day. She had, of course, heard about the Maypole, and I wondered if she would come out and watch. I wished there weren't so many papers and cans littered around the place, but we wouldn't have time to clean them all up and set up the Maypole and get the children lined up.

I was slow finishing my last test and was a little late getting home from school. But my big brother and Irving Liebowitz already had set up the Maypole. It did look pretty with its many colored streamers floating in the breeze. All the little neighborhood children were laughing and happy as the big girls were lining them up to take turns dancing around the Maypole. And, would you believe it? Carmelita was hurrying around, picking up papers and trash and stuffing them into the trash baskets.

"We have to have it clean for the little kids," she told me as I came along. Then she asked, "What will make music?"

"We're just going to clap and sing, maybe," I answered. Without waiting for more, Carmelita dashed off and in no time was back with a guitar. She had put on a very wide yellow skirt, a blouse with colored embroidery and many strings of beads.

She sat on a bench and began a gay tune when the first children were ready to dance. We bigger girls were busy helping the little ones wind the streamers in and out. Soon I heard a violin playing, and the Fiola grandfather stood beside Carmelita playing the same tune. My brother came with his harmonica. Someone sang the tune from an open window; and as I looked up I could see May baskets in many windows, in the different big buildings. Agnes and Sylvia and Susie and Lola and Maria all must have been very busy hanging May baskets.

People came out of the buildings to join in the fun of clapping and singing and watching the little Maypole dancers. My father and some of the other men came home from work and watched, smiling. Mother brought Mrs. Schultz down, and they each carried their May baskets.

At last sunset came, and lights began to glow in the buildings. The Maypole dancers were getting tired, but were still happy. Mothers began to lead them into the house for supper. But mostly everyone stood around, talking and laughing together, even people whom I'd never heard laugh before. As Susie went by with her little brother, Carmelita was standing near my parents and me. The little boy said, "That was the best May Day for neighbors. Let's do it again next year."

Carmelita and I said, "Yes, let's do it next year."

My mother and father both looked very happy.

—ROSALYN HARRISON AND MILDRED CORELL LUCKHARDT

# A New England May Day

It was May Day, and I had been wading up the brook after the fragile white blossoms of the shadbush, or sugar pear, as we called it then; for we were that evening to hang our homemade May baskets, filled with flowers, on the front doors of our playmates and neighbors. It was an unusual May Day, I had thought gratefully, as I paddled my way around the slippery rocks and through the cold waters, for it was seldom that the wild cherry and sugar pear were in blossom or even in full bud in time for the hanging of May baskets.

—FROM *The White Gate* BY MARY ELLEN CHASE

# May Day

Good morning, Lords and ladies, it is the first of May;
We hope you'll view our garland, it is so sweet and gay.

The cuckoo sings in April, the cuckoo sings in May,
The cuckoo sings in June, in July she flies away.

The cuckoo drinks cold water to make her sing so clear.
And then she sings "Cuckoo! Cuckoo!" for three months in the year.

I love my little brother and sister every day,
But I seem to love them better in the merry month of May.

—OLD SONG

# Spring

Now do a choir of chirping minstrels bring
In triumph to the world the youthful spring!
The valleys, hills, and woods, in rich array,
Welcome the coming of the longed-for May.

—THOMAS CAREW

# Queen of the May

"I wonder who'll make a May party this year," said Gertie.

"I don't know. Nobody asked me yet," Charlotte replied.

"We ought to make one ourselves," Henny suggested.

"That's a marvelous idea!" Sarah cried enthusiastically. "With Ella in charge, it would be the fanciest May party anybody ever saw!"

"Thanks," Ella answered, "but do you realize how much work a May party is?"

"We could all help," Sarah said coaxingly.

"Well—," Ella hesitated. The sisters could tell the idea was catching on. "It would be a lot of fun."

Charlotte clapped her hands together. "Oh, Ella, who'll be the Queen? Who'll be the Queen of the May?"

Gertie jumped up and down. "Ooh! I want to be the Queen!"

"I'm sorry," Ella told them, "but you're too little to be the Queen, both of you."

Their disappointment lasted only a moment, for by now Ella's imagination was running riot. "Gertie, you could be a little green elf with a peaked cap. And I'll twist strips of green and brown crepe paper for a belt. You'd be the cutest thing!"

"If I can't be the Queen, could I be a fairy, Ella?" Charlotte burst in. "With big silver wings on my back? I'd like that!"

"Yes," Ella considered. "A silver band on your head, maybe. It would look nice against your brown hair."

"Not me," Henny replied quickly. "I'm much too grown up. I'll help Ella with the managing. You be the Queen, Sarah."

"Maybe one of the girls who join us will want to be Queen."

"Since we're making it, I think it's only fair that somebody in our family should be Queen."

"Besides," Ella continued, "there are all kinds of other wonderful things they could be."

And that's how Sarah got to be Queen of the May.

The ten days that followed were filled with activity. The children combed the neighborhood. "Want to join our May party?" they asked friends and relatives. "It costs only ten cents to pay for the costumes."

Ella kept strict account of the money that came in, and soon she was able to report that they already had twenty dimes. "Wow!" exclaimed Gertie, "twenty children! And don't forget there's us too!"

"Yes," said Ella. "I think that ought to be enough. Let's not ask anybody else. We'll have an awful lot to do as it is."

Every afternoon, Mama's kitchen seemed to burst at the seams with children of the neighborhood. Children of all shapes and sizes stopped by for fittings and remained to cut and twist, pin and stitch, color and paste, all under artist Ella's direction. Crowns and wings and flowers, hats and wands and belts, rapidly came into being. It was just as Mama said, "Many hands make work light." Some of the other mamas pitched in too. Even Lena took to dropping in evenings to lend an expert sewing hand.

Papa went to work with his carpenter tools and fashioned a

Maypole. It had a broomstick handle for the pole and a wooden hoop from a sugar barrel for its wheel-like top. Ella wound strips of white, pink, and blue paper around the pole and crisscrossed them over the hoop. Next many colored streamers and dainty flower rosettes were hung from it. When at last Ella had finished, everyone agreed it was a miracle of loveliness.

The night before, everything was ready. "There," Ella said with satisfaction as she twisted the last leaf into the garland of flowers for Queen Sarah's head. "Try it on, Sarah." She eyed her thoughtfully. "It doesn't look right with braids. You'll have to wear your hair loose tomorrow."

"I know," agreed Sarah. "It has to be loose. If only it was curly like Henny's," she added wishfully.

Lena spoke up. "If Mama says it's all right, I could make you lovely curls first thing in the morning. I just bought a marvelous curling iron!"

"But doesn't it hurt the hair?" Mama asked doubtfully.

"No. You just have to be a little careful. Don't worry. I know how to use it. Sarah will have curls just as nice as Henny's, you'll see."

The eventful day dawned, blue-skied, sunny, and warm. Lena arrived bright and early with the curling iron, and the family gathered around to watch as she went to work. First she lit the gas stove and thrust the long iron into the blue flame. In a few moments she pulled it out, testing its heat by twirling it swiftly in the air. "Now, Sarah," she cautioned, "stand perfectly still." Hiss-s-s! the iron steamed as Lena skillfully wound a small bunch of Sarah's hair over and over up toward the scalp. Sarah held her breath. Would it really make a curl? Now slowly, carefully the hair was being unwound.

There it was—a long, thick, perfect curl! "Oh, Sarah, it's just gorgeous!" Charlotte cried. Sarah's fingers reached up timidly as if fearful that the magic curl would disappear at her touch. It was true! It was real! Round and smooth and shapely. "Oh, Lena! Let's hurry and do the rest!"

When it was over, Sarah raced to the bedroom mirror. She stared at herself. Was this stranger Sarah? Slowly she turned her head, studying herself from all angles. Lena put a mirror in her hand so she could see the back of her head as well. It was thrilling to feel the long blonde curls bob against her cheeks, her shoulders, her back! Starry-eyed, she threw her arms around Lena. "Thanks a million, billion times!"

Henny was mystified. "Such a fuss about curly hair! Wait till tomorrow when it'll be all tangled up. You won't be so overjoyed then when you have to comb and brush it out."

Right after lunch, Ella jumped up and clapped her hands. "Listen, everybody. Now's the time! Get dressed, and we'll meet the others downstairs."

"That's right," Mama approved. "If they all come tramping in here, it'll be a madhouse."

Such a flurry and to-do! But everything went according to plan. Soon the Queen, followed by a dazzling fairy and a quaint elf, was standing impatiently in front of the house. Charlie was there too, dressed as a small Uncle Sam in red, white, and blue, with a cardboard hat tilted rakishly on his head.

Now other fairy-book folk appeared. There was Red Riding Hood approaching, hand in hand with Little Boy Blue. Here came a red devil and a scary witch in black. Close behind followed a little Dutch girl in white cap and apron with a blond Dutch boy for her partner. Soon the street was a-sparkle with all the colors of the rainbow.

Ella cupped her hands. "Line up, everybody!" she shouted. Two by two the children fell into place, with Queen Sarah standing proudly at their head. As she held the beribboned Maypole aloft, her curls caught the gold of the afternoon sun. Lena turned to Mama with a smile. "With such curls, she feels like a real Queen."

Henny ran up and down the line to see if everything was in order. "Forward, march!" Ella gave the command. The glittering array moved down the street, past the crowd of admiring spectators. At the very end of the line rolled several gaily decorated carts containing the smallest children. Last of all came Charlie. He stood up in his red, white, and blue wagon waving with his cane at the curious little outsiders who trotted along behind.

"Sit down!" Henny ordered, "or you'll fall!"

They were about halfway to the park when a gray patch of cloud fell across the sun. A sudden gust of wind set costumes rustling. Anxiously Ella scanned the sky. It grew darker. The wind rose, scattering dust and papers before it. The Maypole swayed back perilously. Sarah had to hold on with all her might. There was a rumble of thunder, and a few blobs of rain spattered the marchers. "My costume will get all melted!" a little girl lamented. The drops grew heavier.

"Oh, how awful" Henny cried despairingly. "Ella, what'll we do?"

Ella stood still, thinking hard. Then it came to her. She knew what to do. Her arm shot forward. "This way, everybody. Turn left!" she shouted. "Double quick time!" One, two—one, two!"

In less time than it takes to tell, the whole parade, Maypole, carts, children, and all had disappeared into Papa's shop. Just in the nick of time, too! Cr-a-ack! A sharp clap of thunder bounced over the rooftops, and the rain pelted down in torrents.

Papa was in the back making up a rag bale when the army of youngsters swooped down upon him. He jumped out of the bin and came running. "What's this?" he shouted above the din.

"It started raining, and we were nearby. And I had to save the costumes!" explained Ella.

"Raining! Oh, my!" Papa passed his fingers through his hair. All about him were long faces. "It's really a shame," he said sympathetically.

"The ground will be all soaking and full of puddles!" Queen Sarah was close to tears.

"And we were going to dance around the Maypole and everything," Gertie said, whimpering. In another second, the other smaller children had joined in, loudly wailing their disappointment.

"Stop yammering!" Ella yelled. "We can still have our May party. We'll have it right here. That is—" she turned questioningly— "if it's all right with my papa."

Ella could see that Papa wasn't exactly pleased. But with a host of little boys and girls staring up at him pleadingly, he just couldn't say no. "Well, what with the rain, there won't be any business. The peddlers will be coming in anyway, so I couldn't do much work." A grin was slowly spreading across his face as if he too were being caught up by the party spirit. "Come on, Queen Sarah! On your throne!" He lifted her up in his strong arms and perched her high on his rolltop desk.

Pulling off the lid of the empty pot-bellied stove, he stuck the Maypole inside. It looked so comical there, the children shrieked with laughter. "The stove's got an umbrella!" a little boy cried out.

"Clear the center!" Ella called out. She and Henny pulled the chairs away from the stove and backed them up against the walls. Papa brought out boxes, old newspaper bundles, and piles of rag sacks. "Sit down, everybody!" ordered Ella, and there was a mad scramble for places.

No sooner was everyone seated than the peddlers came straggling in. All wet and be draggled, they stared around bewilderedly. "Say, Pop, you make the school?" peddler Joe wanted to know.

"Join the party!" everyone greeted the newcomers.

"But I ain't dressed up!" Picklenose moaned with comical sadness. A little boy ran forward and yielded up a gold paper crown. Picklenose promptly balanced it on the top of his head. "Don't I look fancy?" he exclaimed, swaggering up and down.

Ella struck up a song. "Today's the first of May, May, May! Today's the first of May!" coaxing everyone to join. Joe pulled out a battered harmonica from a pocket and played along. The air was filled with music as one rousing tune followed another with different youngsters standing up to lead.

Then Scotty took the center of the floor. "Watch this, kids!" he roared. He danced a lively sailor's hornpipe. The delighted children clapped their hands and beat out the rhythm with their feet. When the dance was over, they clamored for more. Scotty was puffing hard and mopping his brow. "I guess I ain't as spry as I used to be," he apologized. "So, with your Highness's permission, Queen Sarah, I'd like to sit me down."

Polack made a face. "Bah! You call that a dance! I show you real dance—Polish dance. Joe, you play the song—you know—the one I already teach you." He grabbed hold of Henny's arm and began to hop and leap about, yelling out the steps to her. The pair turned and twisted and flew all around the basement as the children screamed with delight. The dance ended with Polack twirling Henny high in the air. "Now that's what I call a dance!" he said proudly, as he bowed to the loud applause.

Now Queen Sarah clapped her hands. "Ladies of my court, let the Maypole dance begin!"

Picklenose jumped up eagerly. "Seeing as I still got my crown on, I'll hold the Maypole." He lifted it high. The bigger girls formed a circle and took hold of the streamers. In and out and under they waltzed, winding the ribbons in pretty patterns around the pole. This time it was the peddlers who did the applauding. They stamped their feet and whistled.

Charlotte sprang on a chair. "Listen, everybody!" she cried, "why don't we have a play, since we're all wearing costumes!"

Everyone was enraptured with the idea. "Tell us a story, Charlotte. Then we can act it out," they cried. The room grew quiet as Charlotte began to make up a play. But she didn't get very far. Every head turned toward the staircase. A very wet pair of shoes was squeaking—squidge, squidge, squidge—down the steps.

"So this is where you are," an excited voice hailed them. It was Uncle Hyman, all soaked and dripping. "I was running all over the park looking for you!" He waved his hands at them. "Now, please, everybody, don't get lost again. Wait right here till I come back!" Loudly the shoes squidged up the stairs again, leaving a wet trail behind them.

Papa shrugged his shoulders. "Where's that meshugener (crazy one) going?"

"Go on with the play, Charlotte," urged one of the elves.

Charlotte considered a moment. "Well, now let's see. Where was I. Oh—"

The squidgy sounds were heard again, only slower this time. Uncle Hyman appeared, arms laden with two bulging paper bags. He staggered over to Sarah and set the bags down on the desk. "See what I got!"

The youngsters bounded out of their seats and milled around the Queen. Sarah thrust her hand inside one of the bags and came up with something. With a big smile, she held it up for all to see. There was a tremendous shout. "Ice cream sandwiches!" A forest of eager hands stretched forward to receive the surprise. "Gimme one!" "Gimme one!" Six active hands popped furiously in and out of the bags as Henny and Ella rushed to Sarah's rescue. Luckily there was enough for everyone, including the peddlers. As the youngsters bit into the crisp cracker covering, a boy cried out, "Gee, this is the best part of all. Thanks a lot; Mr. Uncle."

That reminded the others of their manners, and thank-yous for Uncle Hyman came flying from every side.

You could see Uncle Hyman was pleased, but he waved his hands to shush them. "So stop thanking me already and eat," he spluttered. "The ice cream will melt."

A golden shaft of light suddenly spread across the cellar steps. "Look, the sun's out!" someone cried.

"Now it shines," observed Papa. "Just when the party's over."

"Well, at least we'll be able to march back without spoiling our costumes," Ella declared. "Line up, all of you, as we were in the beginning."

There was a hustle and bustle. Then like a dazzling rainbow, the column of masqueraders filed up the stairs and out into the sunshine.

"Did you ever hear of a May party in a cellar?" the witch said to Puss-in-Boots.

"I'm glad it rained!" exclaimed Little Bo-Peep. "It was the best May party ever."

And everyone agreed.

—SYDNEY TAYLOR

# The Minstrel Song

Once, long, long ago, there lived in a country over the sea a king called Rene, who married a lovely princess named Imogene. She came across the seas to the king's beautiful country, and all his people welcomed her with great joy because the king loved her.

"What can I do to please thee today?" the king asked her every morning; and one day she answered that she would like to hear all the minstrels in the king's country, for they were said to be the finest in the world.

As soon as the king heard this, he called his heralds and sent them everywhere through his land to sound the trumpets and call aloud: "Hear, ye minstrels! King Rene, our gracious king, bids ye come to the court on May Day, for love of the Queen Imogene."

The minstrels were men who sang beautiful songs and played on harps; and long ago they went about from place to place, from castle to castle, from palace to cottage, and were always sure of a welcome wherever they roamed. They could sing of the brave deeds that the knights had done and of wars and battles. They could tell of mighty hunters who hunted in the great forests, and of fairies and goblins, better than a storybook. And because there were no storybooks in those days, everybody from little children to the king was glad to see them come.

So when the minstrels heard the king's message they made haste to the palace on May Day; and it so happened that some of them met on the way and decided to travel together. One of these minstrels was a young man named Harmonius; and while the others talked of the songs they would sing he gathered wild flowers by the roadside.

"I can sing of drums and battles," said the oldest minstrel, whose hair was white and whose step was slow.

"I can sing of ladies and their fair faces," said the youngest minstrel; but Harmonius whispered, "Listen! Listen!"

"Oh, we hear nothing but the wind in the treetops," said the others. "We have no time to stop and listen."

Then they hurried on and left Harmonius; and he stood under the trees and listened, for he heard something very sweet. At last he knew that it was the wind singing of its travels through the wide world, telling how it raced over the blue sea, tossing the waves and rocking the white ships, and hurried on to the hills where all the flowers danced gayly in time to the tune. Harmonious could understand every word:

> Nobody follows me where I go,
> Over the mountains or valleys below;
> Nobody sees where the wild winds blow,
> Only the Father in Heaven can know.

That was the chorus of the wind's song. Harmonius listened until he knew the whole song from beginning to end; and then he ran on and soon reached his friends, who were talking of the grand sights they would see.

"We shall see the king and speak to him," said the oldest of the minstrels.

"And his golden crown and the queen's jewels," added the youngest; and Harmonius had no chance to tell of the wind's song, although he thought about it time and time again.

Now their path led through the wood; and Harmonius said, "Hush! Listen!" But the others answered, "Oh, that is only the sound of the brook trickling over stones. Let us haste to the king's court."

But Harmonius stayed to hear the song the brook was singing, of journeying through mosses and ferns and shady ways and of tumbling over rocks in shining waterfalls on its way to the sea.

> Rippling and bubbling through shade and sun,
> On to the beautiful sea I run;
> Singing forever though none be near,
> For God in Heaven can always hear.

sang the little brook. Harmonius listened until he knew every word of the song and then hurried on.

When he reached the others they still talked of the king and queen, so he could not tell them of the brook. As they talked he heard something again that was wonderfully sweet, and he cried "Listen! Listen!"

"Oh, that is only a bird!" the others replied. "Let us haste to the king's court!"

But Harmonius would not go, for the bird sang so joyfully that Harmonius laughed aloud. It was singing of green trees, and in every tree a nest, and in every nest eggs!

> Merrily, merrily, listen to me,
> Flitting and flying from tree to tree,

Nothing fear I, by land or sea,
For God in Heaven is watching me.

"Thank you, little bird," said Harmonius, "you have taught me a song." And he made haste to join his comrades, for by this time they were near the palace.

When they had gone in, they received a hearty welcome and were feasted in the great hall before they came before the king. The king and queen sat on their thrones together. The king thought of the queen and the minstrels; but she thought of her old home and butterflies she had chased as a child.

One by one the minstrels played before them. The oldest sang of battles and drums, as he had said he would; the youngest sang of ladies and their fair faces, which pleased the court ladies very much.

Then came Harmonius. And when he touched his harp and sang, the song sounded like the wind blowing, the sea roaring, and the trees creaking; then it grew soft and sounded like a trickling brook dripping on stones and running over little pebbles; and while the king and queen and all the court listened in surprise, Harmonius' song grew sweeter, sweeter, as if you heard all the birds in Spring. Then the song ended.

The queen clapped her hands; the ladies waved their handerchiefs; the king came down form his throne to ask Harmonius if he came from Fairyland with such a wonderful song. But Harmonius answered:

"Three singers sang along our way,
And I learned the song from them today."

The other minstrels looked up in surprise; and the oldest said to the king, "Harmonius is dreaming! We heard no music on our way today." And the youngest said, "Harmonius is surely mad! We met nobody on our way today."

The queen said, "This is an old, old song. I heard it from the wind and the water and the birds when I was a little child. Harmonius shall be our court minstrel and sing to us every day of this great, wide, wonderful, beautiful world."

—MAUD LINDSAY

# Tree Voices (in Australia)

When bush-fire clouds of pollen
   Blow from the creeks in spring,
In friendly rows of native pine
   The birds all meet to sing.
—LINES FROM *Tree Voices* BY IRENE GOUGH

# Billy and Fats Go Round the Maypole

The winter was hardly over when Miss Dowd announced that it was time to start practicing for the May Day program.

"May Day already," Billy whispered to Fats. "And there's still some old dirty snow outside."

"Hey nonny nonny, ugh," whispered Fats.

Billy and Fats had been having their troubles with May Day for years. In kindergarten, they had had to dress up in purple crepe and be two cute little crocuses. Ever since they had been working on ways to get out of dancing on May Day, but they hadn't come up with anything reliable yet.

Well, this year Miss Dowd's room was to do the Maypole dance, and Miss Dowd got right to work, rehearsing them in the gym. Later, when the weather warmed up, they would rehearse outdoors, with a real Maypole, with real streamers on it.

Billy and Fats had never worked themselves to death learning the dances before, because they always had partners. Naturally the partners were girls, and naturally the girls learned all the steps right away and liked it. So it never mattered how many mistakes Billy

297

and Fats made as long as they kept moving and ended up facing the right partner.

This Maypole business was different. They had partners, all right, and there was a little bowing and curtsying and stuff at the beginning of the dance. Then the girls all went one way around the Maypole, and the boys went on the other, so the boys were strictly on their own.

And every time anybody made a mistake, **even a little** one, the streamers got all tangled up and Miss Dowd **stopped the music**. Then they had to untangle the streamers. This wasn't as simple as it sounds, either, especially if the wind was blowing.

Worst of all, when the streamers were all untangled down to the one that was wrong, that one generally turned out to have Billy or Fats on the end of it. Well, Miss Dowd got crosser and crosser and worked them harder and harder, but nothing much came of it. It was the week before May Day, and still they had never once wound all the streamers up, and unwound them again, without stopping at least once to untangle.

By then it was time for elections, and it was Miss Dowd's room's turn to elect the May Queen. That meant another room would elect the May King, and the rest of the rooms, their attendants.

Every year there was a lot of talk by the teachers about voting for whoever had the finest character, but every year the best-looking ones got elected just the same. Billy and Fats had never paid much attention to the elections, because they were never in any danger of being elected, for either their good looks or their fine characters.

So Fats was surprised when he heard Billy ask Gus Schultz, "Who are you voting for, for May Queen?"

"Carol Jones, I guess," said Gus. "You got any better ideas?"

"Well, I sort of thought of Sandra Riley," said Billy.

"Sandra Riley!" squawked Gus.

"Sure. She's pretty nice, for a girl. She can run faster than any kid in the room."

"Yeah, sure, but for *May Queen*? With those carroty pigtails and skinny legs?"

"Listen, what difference does it make?" demanded Billy. "Carol Jones will get it anyway, but Carol Jones is a pain in the neck to me, so why should I vote for her? Besides, Sandra would be ticked to death to get a few votes."

"I guess you're right," admitted Gus. "Say, maybe I'll vote for Sandra, too."

Then Billy cornered Peggy Crowley and Ann Meyers on the playground. "Well, I guess Carol Jones is all set to be Queen of the May," he said cheerfully.

"If she gets elected," snorted Peggy.

"What do you mean, if?" asked Billy. "She's the prettiest girl in the room, isn't she?"

"*She* certainly thinks so," sniffed Ann. "And I suppose all the boys will vote for her. They always do."

"Oh, I dunno," mumbled Billy. "Gus Schultz was just saying he might vote for Sandra Riley."

"Did he, no kidding?" asked Peggy.

"Sure he did," replied Billy. "Not that it'll make any difference. Carol's a cinch to get elected."

"Oh, she is, is she?" demanded Peggy. "We'll see about that."

After Billy had talked to a few more kids, Fats asked suspiciously, "Hey, what's the big idea, anyway?"

"Nothing," replied Billy. "It's a free country, isn't it?" And that was all Fats could get out of him.

Well, the next day they had the election, and after all the slips were collected and counted, Sandra Riley had seven more votes than Carol Jones and was elected May Queen.

Sandra was so pleased and surprised she nearly cried, and Carol was very nice about it nad congratulated her. Miss Dowd said it was a fine choice, and now would the class please file out quietly to the Maypole and try to get it right this time. So there they were, right back at the Maypole again. Miss Dowd started the music and then stopped it suddenly.

"Dear me, I forgot," she said. "Sandra, will you please step out? You won't be in the dance now, of course. There will be a rehearsal for the May King and Queen and their attendants tomorrow. Now then, class, all together now, *one* and *two* and—"

But Billy just stood still, holding the end of his stream. "Please, Miss Dowd," he called over the music, "what do I do now? I don't have a partner."

"Oh, of course!" exclaimed Miss Dowd. "Sandra was your partner, wasn't she? I'm afraid you won't be able to be in the dance either, then."

Well, of course Fats saw it all now. He was just about fit to be tied, especially when he remembered how he had let Billy talk him into voting for Sandra. But he just had to stand there and take it, while Miss Dowd told Billy not to be disappointed, because he could be a big help passing out programs.

Fats felt a whole lot worse when he found out what he had to wear. The girls were to be all dolled up fit to kill, and they just loved it. The boys, even Billy, had to wear long white pants. But all the boys in the dance had to wear sashes, too, to match the streams they held. Fats's streamer was bright pink.

So May Day morning, Fats's mother tied a big pink sash around his middle and told him to be careful not to rumple it. As soon as he got out of the house, Fats wadded up the sash and stuffed it into his pocket. At school, there were dozens of kids milling around in costumes, mostly crepe paper coming part at the seams.

Fats eased into the building, and in the hall ran into Billy, looking very important with a stack of programs. Fats walked right by without speaking.

Just then Miss Dowd and the principal, Miss Griswold, darted out of the office and grabbed hold of Billy and started talking to him. Fats quietly backtracked a little, to see what was going on. Miss Dowd was saying to Billy, "The teachers know more about what goes on around this school than you children think we do."

Well, this didn't sound too good for Billy, or for anybody else that happened to be around, either. Fats was glad that he could just start walking any time he wanted to. Miss Dowd went on to say that she knew all along that Billy was the one responsible for getting Sandra elected May Queen. She thought it was just wonderful of him, because nobody deserved to be May Queen more than Sandra.

Fats couldn't figure out what all this was leading up to, but he soon found out. Jim Haskin, from Miss Kemp's room, had been elected May King. But Jim's mother had just phoned to say he had a temperature of 102 this morning and couldn't possibly come to school.

"So Miss Dowd and I have both agreed that nobody deserves the honor more than you do. So we are asking you to take Jim's part in the ceremony today!" Miss Griswold explained to Billy.

"But I don't—I can't—I mean, it ought to be somebody out of Miss Kemp's room!" stuttered Billy. "Anyway, I wouldn't even know what to do."

"It's perfectly simple. You won't have a bit of trouble," said Miss Griswold kindly. "Jimmy's robes and crown will just fit you."

"Robes?" said Billy in a hollow voice. "Crown?"

"Yes they're in my office. Come along and we'll explain everything."

Billy was still repeating, "I couldn't *honest*, I couldn't—" when Miss Dowd and Miss Griswold led him firmly into the office and shut the door.

Fats went out and took his place with the rest of the class at the edge of the lawn. The folding chairs were filling up with mothers and a few fathers with movie cameras and lots of wiggling little brothers and sisters. Fats saw his own mother with his baby brother. She waved at him and made faces until he remembered the sash in his pocket. So he got it out and tied it on again.

Then the music started, and the May King and Queen appeared in the big front doorway of the school. Fats hardly recognized Sandra. She looked perfectly beautiful in a long white dress that hid her skinny legs. Her hair was brushed out loose around her shoulders, and it glittered in the sun like polished copper.

But Fats didn't have any trouble recognizing Billy. There he stood, with a wide blue sash around his middle, wearing a sort of blue velvet cape that hung down behind and dragged on the ground. On his head, he balanced a wobbly crown like a basket of eggs.

Then the music changed to a march, and Sandra started gracefully down the steps. After a bit, Billy started too. It looked to Fats as if somebody had pushed him from behind. He caught up with Sandra, and they started the long march to the thrones at the far end of the lawn, followed by the attendants, two by two. Last of all came a little kindergarten kid carrying a wreath of flowers on a pillow.

Either everybody else was out of step, or Billy was. Fats decided it was probably Billy. And Fats knew that, in about three

minutes, Billy was going to have to put that wreath of flowers on Sandra's head without putting her eye out, and with four hundred people watching him. Altogether, Fats couldn't remember when he had had a better time at a May Day Program.

Gus Schultz, standing next to Fats, whispered in his ear, "Hey! I thought Jim Haskin was May King. What's Billy Kidwell doing out there?"

"Jim's sick," explained Fats. "So they picked Billy."

"Why Billy?" asked Gus.

"Oh, didn't you hear?" said Fats. "It was on account of his fine character."

—MARION HOLLAND

# A Dime's Worth, for Free

Billy Kidwell didn't mind arithmetic so much when it was just plain numbers but, in the book they were using this year, you never knew when you would come across a couple of feeble-minded characters named A and B. In the beginning of the book, A was always buying potatoes by the bushel and selling them to B by the peck, and simple stuff like that, but along toward the end they got more ambitious.

Today, for instance. It was the first really hot day of spring, and the windows were open, letting in a lot of fine, interesting smells—and here were A and B again. This time they seemed to be messing around with a stream that had a current of two miles per hour. Well, Billy could think of plenty of sensible things he and Fats could do with a stream like that on a day like this. But not Mr. A. and Mr. B. Oh no, they had to get themselves a couple of rowboats, one apiece, and start rowing in opposite directions. Now Billy was supposed to figure out how far apart they would be after A had rowed upstream for fifty minutes and B had rowed downstream for an hour and a quarter.

As if any body cared. Fats Martin, across the aisle, didn't seem to care, either. Neither did anybody else; at least, when Miss Dowd collected the papers almost all the answers were different, and all of them were wrong.

Well, Miss Dowd just blew up. You might have thought she would have put some of the blame where it belonged, on A and B. Or on the weather coming in through the windows and making everybody just itch to get outside. But no, she gave them a long lecture, about how if this was the best they could do, it was time they all went back and had a good drill on Basic Fundamentals. Then she covered the whole front blackboard with long columns of figures, to be copied down and added up for homework.

At three o'clock, Billy and Fats left school together in silence. The sun was still hot, and the breeze still smelled of wet dirt and plum trees in bloom, but the whole day was ruined.

"It'll take an hour, anyway, to do all that homework," said Billy finally, aiming a kick at a stone.

"Or two hours," said Fats gloomily.

"If not three," groaned Billy. He folded his homework paper as small as possible and stuck it in his jacket. His fingers found a dime he had forgotten, and he fished it out. "Say, let's go down to Schultz's and get a couple of dill pickles," he said.

"Or jelly beans," suggested Fats, who had not earned his name on a diet of dill pickles.

Schultz's Delicatessen was cool and dark and smelled of pickles and cinnamon and new magazines. Around the first of the month, there was usually quite a crowd around the magazine rack; for two cents' worth of lemon drops, a fast reader could get through a dollar's worth of magazines in an afternoon. Mr. Schultz was always threatening to take the magazines out, but he never did.

Today the place was empty. All the magazines were old and limp looking, and there wouldn't be any new ones in for at least a week.

"Well, gentlemen, what can I do for you?" asked Mr. Schultz, the way he always did.

Billy and Fats were still arguing. Dill pickles were two for a dime, but they were six cents apiece, so if Billy bought a dill pickle, Fats would only have four cents left for jelly beans, which could be divided evenly, even if they had to count them and break the last one in half.

On the other hand, Billy pointed out, whose dime was it, anyway?

Then the phone rang, and Mr. Schultz answered it; and after a minute Billy and Fats quit arguing to listen. Mr. Schultz's red face got redder and redder, his white moustache bristled, and he shouted so loud they couldn't understand one single word he was saying, except that it was something about Emil. Emil was Mr. Schultz's grandson, who drove the delivery truck.

Finally Mr. Schultz slammed the phone down and put both hands up to his head and groaned.

"What's the matter?" asked Billy in alarm. "Is Emil sick?"

"No!" roared Mr. Schultz. "But he will be, when I get hold of him! Twice already he parks the truck by a fireplug, and the police warn him. Now he does it again, and they take him to the station house and the truck along with him. So now I got to go pay the fine before they let him go. If I don't go, who makes the afternoon deliveries? Nobody, that's who!" He took off his white apron and threw it on the floor and jammed his hat on the back of his head.

"So hurry up!" he shouted. "Pickles or jelly beans, I don't care which, but make up your minds. I got to lock up."

"Jelly beans," said Billy hastily. Mr. Schultz weighed them out, rang up the dime on the cash register, and shooed them toward the door.

It was then that Billy had his big idea. "Look, Mr. Schultz, he said eagerly, "we'll mind the store for you; won't we, Fats? I bet we know the price of everything in here. Don't we, Fats?"

"We ought to," mumbled Fats, his mouth full of jelly beans.

Mr. Schultz rubbed his nose and looked doubtful. "What's the matter?" asked Billy. "Don't you trust us with your money?"

"Sure, sure," said Mr. Schultz. "I know you boys. With my money I trust you like my own self. But . . ." His eyes swept doubtfully over the candy bars and salted peanuts, over the glass case of pickles and spiced ham and cheese. "All right," he said finally. "And look, when I get back, I give you a dime's worth for free, each, anything you want. But not till I get back—OK?"

"OK," they agreed, and Mr. Schultz hurried out, muttering something about Emil under his breath.

"A dime's worth for free," cried Fats. "Come on, let's pick it out."

But Billy headed straight for the cash register. "We got to hurry," he said. "Mr. Schultz will be back any minute, or somebody might come in."

Fats's round pink face turned pale. "Hey," he said hoarsely, "have you gone crazy? What you doing with that cash register?"

"Homework," replied Billy, pulling the paper out of his pocket. "Look here. You punch the keys for each number, and after you punch off the whole problem, you punch the key marked total, and the answer jumps up, all added up. See?"

Fats saw. "Hot diggety," he remarked in awe. "But look, it comes out in dollars and cents. What about that?"

Billy was already punching, marking his place on the paper

with his thumb. "Doesn't matter. This thing'll add up to $99.99, so we can get any answer under ten thousand, and I don't think any of them are going-to be that high. The problems are long, but the numbers aren't so big. Watch." He finished the first problem and punched the key marked Total. A bell rang, the number $87.92 jumped up—and the cash drawer shot out and hit him in the stomach.

"Ouch," he yelled. Then he copied down the answer—8,792.

"Let me do the next," begged Fats.

But Billy was already working at it, standing back a respectful distance from the cash drawer. "Nope. I got the hang of it now. You watch the door. We don't want anybody busting in."

Billy got faster and faster as he went along, copying off each answer as the register added it up. Fats watched the door. A very little girl came in with a nickel and spent a long time deciding on two peppermint sticks. Billy rang up a nickel between problems.

He was going great guns now. Fats got bored watching the door, and wandered around, trying to figure out what to take a dime's worth of, for free. He looked in the soft drink cooler—root beer, ginger ale, orange pop. No raspberry. He poked among the wooden cases in the back, where Mr. Schultz kept the pop, until he got around to putting it in the cooler. He dragged up a couple of empties to stand on, to see what was in the top case.

Billy was ringing up the last problem when a little man came in. In spite of the heat, the little man had his collar turned up, and his hands in his pockets. He drifted over to the candy case and glanced toward the rear of the store, where Fats was hidden by a pile of boxes.

Billy punched the *total* key, the bell rang, and the cash drawer popped open. Billy reached for his pencil to copy down the last answer.

"Leave it open, kid," said a gruff voice. "This is a stickup, see?"

It was just like the movies. With one hand still in his pocket, the man reached across and scooped all the bills out of the cash drawer. It seemed to Billy that this must be happening to somebody else. He looked around for a weapon, but there was nothing within reach but a glass jar of lollipops and some bags of pretzels. "Hey," he said feebly, "you can't do that. Mr. Schultz won't like it. Hey, Fats!" he shouted.

"Shuddup," snarled the little man as if he meant it. Billy shut up. Fats, balanced on a pile of boxes with a bottle of raspberry pop in each hand, heard his name and looked toward the front of the store. The sight that met his eyes unbalanced him completely. The boxes shifted under his feet, and he let go of one bottle to grab for support. The bottle hit the cement floor and exploded, With a yell, Fats dropped the other bottle. The two explosions echoed like gunshots.

The little man whirled to face the rear of the store, and shouted, "Drop that gun—I got you covered!"

This was too much for Fats. He lost his balance and fell, bringing down with him a cascade of pop bottles. It sounded like machinegun fire, and the howl of anguish and surprise that Fats let out when he hit the floor sounded like nothing human.

The holdup man turned and ran for the front door. With great presence of mind, Billy threw the glass jar of lollipops at his retreating back. It missed, and shattered against the side of the door, scattering a shower of red, green, and yellow lollipops, just as the door opened and Mr. Schultz and Emil and Officer Maloney walked in.

The holdup man plunged head first into Officer Maloney's wide blue middle.

"Look out!" yelled Billy. "He's got a gun!"

After that, everything was pretty confused for a few minutes. Mr. Schultz was wringing his hands and shouting, "What's going on here? What's going on here?" and Billy was explaining that it was a stickup, and Officer Maloney had handcuffs on the man and was going through his pockets, pulling out a gun and one-dollar bills and five-dollar bills and ten-dollar bills. And every time anybody moved, their feet scrunched on broken glass and lollipops.

Right in the middle of it, Fats staggered up to the front of the store with his shirt front all red and red drops splattering from his hair and the tips of his fingers.

"Get a doctor!" roared Mr. Schultz. "He's shot!"

"Am I?" asked Fats faintly and held up one dripping hand. He licked a finger. "No, it's raspberry pop."

"*My* raspberry pop," groaned Mr. Schultz, noticing the mess in the back of the store for the first time.

Billy and Fats were pretty pleased when it turned out that it was Emil that had to stay and clean up the wreckage, because they were witnesses and had to go with Mr. Schultz and Officer Maloney and the prisoner to the station house. There they had to tell the whole story over and over, and people kept interrupting to ask questions while the sergeant at the desk wrote it all down. In the end, somehow, the sergeant seemed to get the idea that Fats had exploded the bottles on purpose to scare the holdup man away, and that Billy had kept him from making a getaway by stunning him with a jar of lollipops.

Anyway, the police, and even Mr. Schultz, seemed to think that they had done all right, and pretty soon they began to think so themselves.

"Hey, how does it feel to be a hero?" whispered Billy to Fats.

By the time it was all over, Billy was anxious to get home and start acting like a hero. But suddenly Fats had to remember the dime's worth, for free, that they never got, so when Mr. Schultz and Officer Maloney went back to the delicatessen, they went along, too!

Emil had done a pretty good job of cleaning up, considering; and Billy and Fats looked over the shelves and counters while Mr. Schultz checked the cash register with Officer Maloney. They could hear Mr. Schultz start to sputter, but they didn't pay any attention until Officer Maloney called to them.

"Looks as if you boys did a pretty brisk business here while Mr. Schultz was gone," he said, looking at them in a rather peculiar fashion.

"No, sir," said Billy. "Just one nickel's worth of peppermint sticks."

"Then how does it happen that the total on the register shows that somebody sold $6,948.72 worth of merchandise today?" asked Officer Maloney.

Well, then it all came out. Billy showed them the homework

paper, and explained how he had just taken a short cut on the arithmetic homework. "Gosh, sir," he said, squirming, "I never knew the register kept a total of *all* the numbers rung up on it."

Officer Maloney just looked at them for a long, long time, and while he was looking, they began to feel less and less like heroes, and more natural. Finally he said, "Mr. Schultz has to know how much money ought to be in the register, in order to make sure that he gets the right amount back again. Ordinarily he could tell by adding the amount he knows was there last night to the amount the tape says he sold today. I can think of only one way to get this straightened out. You boys take that homework paper, and add together the answers to all the problems. Then take that total, and subtract it from the amount shown on the register tape. Check your answers with each other, and keep right on until you are sure you have them all correct."

He got them each a pencil and a big sheet of paper and pulled two chairs up to the candy counter and cleared a space for them to work. "And when you are quite finished," he said cheerfully. "Mr. Schultz will be delighted to give you each a dime's worth of anything, for free."

"Yes, sir," said Billy and Fats. They sat down and started to work.

"Hey, how does it feel to be a hero?" whispered Fats to Billy.

"Shut up," said Billy.

—MARION HOLLAND

# A Green Plant

At last spring had come to the city. Miguel could tell. Mama opened the windows to talk to the neighbors, and the sunshine felt warm on Miguel's cheeks and arms. He could play ball again with his brother Carlos on the walk in front of the old apartment house.

Best of all, Miguel could sit quietly on the roof—a special, secret place where he could see for blocks, and the noise of cars and street vendors seemed far away. Miguel would sit here dreaming and longing for a juicy summer tomato. How he liked tomatoes!

One day Miguel climbed up to his favorite place to watch buses and cars go by. At last he turned and started to walk away, but he stopped abruptly. At his feet was something small and green. It was a plant growing on his roof! Miguel put his face close to it. He smelled it and touched the leaves. It smelled like tomatoes! How did it get there? Would it grow big and have tomatoes on it? Miguel wanted to care for it—it was his. What a wonderful secret it was!

Every day after school he hurried home to see his green plant. It grew so slowly! One day when Miguel reached the rooftop, some of the leaves on his plant had turned yellow. The next day the yellow leaves were brown and dry. Miguel was worried, yet he did not know whom he could ask for help or advice.

As if in answer to his need, the very next day at school the teacher told the children how plants and trees grow. She showed them the roots that must live in soil. She told them how the plants need sunshine and water. She told them how flowers turn to fruit and the way seeds are formed. Miguel was not sure he understood all these new ideas, but he knew that he must get soil and water for his plant. After school the wind was blowing hard. It made whirlpools of papers along the street. The grocer was busy sweeping the blowing paper when he saw Miguel.

"Boy," he said, "I will pay you if you will help me with these papers."

Miguel did not want to stop. He wanted to hurry to his rooftop. But then he saw the wooden fruit boxes piled near the door.

"May I have a wooden box if I help you?" he asked the grocer.

The grocer scratched his head. What kind of boy was this who wanted a box instead of money? Miguel took the big broom and collected all the papers. He put them into the trash cans near the street. The grocer gave him the wooden box and gratefully added two yellow bananas.

Miguel hurried home. He passed his door quietly and ran to the roof. The plant looked even worse; now he had a box to put it in, but he had no soil. Where could he get soil? How would he bring it to the rooftop?

Miguel remembered last Saturday, when he and Carlos had watched the bulldozers working in a nearby lot. They pushed bricks and great hills of black soil for the dump trucks to haul away. Black soil! Miguel yearned to have some of this soil. The men were still at work when he got there. They laughed when he asked for the soil. "Take all you need," the foreman told Miguel. He filled a large can and carried it home.

Miguel carried his soil up to the roof. He emptied the can, but it filled only the bottom of the box. He needed more. This time he borrowed his mother's bucket. The bucket was heavy when it was full of soil, but it held enough to fill the box. Carefully Miguel lifted his plant out of the crack and buried its long white root in the soil. That night it raised, and the next day Miguel found his plant standing straight and tall. There were even two new green leaves at its top.

When school was out for the summer, Miguel had plenty of time to play handball and tag, to help his mother, and to watch his plant grow. He tied it to a stake for support. It grew clusters of yellow flowers. In each flower a small, green ball slowly formed. As the days passed, they grew larger, and soon the sun and rain turned them red. There were so many tomatoes! Miguel picked one and sucked its warm red juice. Then he picked another and took it to his mother. Now he could tell his secret! Mother was so pleased. She sliced the tomato and put it on a dish on the table. Carlos was really surprised, and Papa could hardly believe it. The next day Mama cooked some tomatoes, and the day after that she cut some into pieces for a salad.

Even after all the tomatoes were gone, Miguel sat on his roof, thinking and planning for next summer. He would help the grocer and get more boxes and seeds. He would find more soil. He would grow more tomatoes. And—he would even grow lettuce and peppers, onions and radishes. Next summer Miguel would have a roof garden.

—FRANCES POTH

# Arbor Day

The date of Arbor Day, or Tree Planters Day, varies in different states and countries; yet families, schools, and garden clubs, and other groups in many places enjoy springtime ceremonies as they plant trees. Conservation Day and Bird Day often are combined with Arbor Day.

On April 10, 1872, in Nebraska, the first Arbor Day in the United States was observed, and more than 1,000,000 trees were planted all over that state on that day. During the next sixteen years more than 350,000,000 trees were planted in Nebraska where before there had been miles of treeless prairies.

J. Sterling Morton, a member of Nebraska's State Board of Agriculture, had promoted the first Arbor Day and had helped with it through the years, and because of him Nebraska has become known as the Tree Planters' State.

Within ten years of Nebraska's first Arbor Day, Ohio and North Dakota held their own Arbor Days, and Connecticut soon joined. On Ohio's first Arbor Day, school children in Cincinnati planted an Author's Grove, naming each tree for a famous person including authors and statesmen.

Since the planting and conservation of trees and forests is important for the welfare and happiness of people, many poems have been written about trees of every kind. Often such poems are read on Arbor Day or Tree Planting Day in many places.

—MILDRED CORELL LUCKHARDT

# 'Tis Merry in the Greenwood

'Tis merry in the greenwood—thus runs the old lay,—
In the gladsome month of lively May,
When wild birds' song on stem and spray
   Invites to forest bower;
Then rears the ash his airy crest,
Then shines the birch in silver vest,
And dark between shows the oak's proud breast,
   Like a chieftain's frowning tower;
Though a thousand branches join their screen,
Yet the broken sunbeams glance between,
And tip the leaves with lighter green,
   With brighter tints the flowers;
Dull is the heart that loves not then
The deep recess of the wildwood glen,
Where roe and red-deer find sheltering den,
   When the sun is in his power.

—SIR WALTER SCOTT

# The Planting of the Apple Tree

What plant we in this apple-tree?
Buds, which the breath of summer days
Shall lengthen into leafy sprays;
Boughs where the thrush, with crimson breast,
Shall haunt, and sing, and hide her nest;
  We plant, upon the sunny lea,
A shadow for the noontide hour,
A shelter from the summer shower,
  When we plant the apple-tree.

What plant we in this apple-tree?
Fruits that shall swell in sunny June,
And redden in the August noon,
And drop, when gentle airs come by,
That fan the blue September sky,
  While children come, with cries of glee,
And seek them where the fragrant grass
Betrays their bed to those who pass,
  At the foot of the apple-tree.

—LINES FROM *"The Planting of the Apple Tree"*

BY WILLIAM CULLEN BRYANT

# Loveliest of Trees

Loveliest of trees, the cherry now
Is hung with bloom along the bough,
And stands about the woodland ride
Wearing white for Eastertide.

Now, of my threescore years and ten,
Twenty will not come again,
And take from seventy springs a score,
It only leaves me fifty more.

And since to look at things in bloom
Fifty springs are little room,
About the woodlands I will go
To see the cherry hung with snow.

—A. E. HOUSMAN

# May Comes to a Saltwater Farm
## on the Maine Coast

May comes in west winds and a sky snowing lambs. The empty barn echoes, but the bay bobs with boats. The world greens in a night, and the cows keep their sweet mouths to the ground all day long. There are snowdrifts in deep dingles and among thick spruces, but there are bluets frosting all other ground. Pussy-paws rise in the pasture, and the mullein pushes out woolen new leaves. The heron arrives from Florida and walks the cove by golden moonlight, thoughtfully, as becomes a much-traveled person. Marbles and hoops roll out on the earth now.

Grandpa hears the first cuckoo. Hepaticas star the hills under leafless trees; the dog-tooth violet hangs the damp valleys with golden bells. Anemones come out in the woods like drops of winter, and they tremble on the faintest breeze. The fish of the month is cod; the reach boat home from sea low with them, but the lobsters keep the man busy at each ebb of the tide. He goes from buoy to buoy, and the young son gets bitten deep by a crab.

The yellow of dandelions burns up like a light on the sky. The girls come home with baskets of wood violets. The old mare brings a handsome colt, all legs, home from the pasture. The columbine hangs her red, gold-lined bells on the cliff too high for the children to reach. The flowers come too fast to keep track of. The shadbush lights the firewoods up like snow; the rhodoras fill the evening swamp with purple smoke. Little boys throw their voices back in their throats and yodel, and other small boys, two farms and a bay away, hear them and answer their spring cry.

One night there is an explosion in all the trees, and people wake up in the morning to a world all new leaves. The bees swarm. The farmer puts on his veiled hat and takes his dip net down, but the bees get into his broad pants, and the little boy laughs to see his father leap out of them and into the bay.

The winds are forever west. The rising sun turns whole forests into singing birds. *Gemini* is the sign, and by Jeminy, the lambs are often twins in the pasture.

Now the plow point goes into earth; the spanned horses come up the fields trampling the bluets, and the plow shines like silver. The father lets the small boy hold the handles of the plow for a round. The potatoes are dropped. The boy scatters the peas. At the end of the day the farmer comes in smelling of cow dressing and good dirt and sits tired in the kitchen by a gingerbread, in peace up to his crinkled eyes.

The light breeze blows the apple blossoms over the dark loam of the garden, for the land is white with apple trees now. Even the deep wild woods light up with pink fires of wild crabapple trees. A man walks through a honeycomb when he walks through a day, and the bees are a faraway thunder to the boy lying lazy, face down in the orchard grass.

School lets out for good, and the boys run the woods like a

parcel of whooping red Indians. The lilacs wall the house round with white fires and purple.

There are sky-blue eggs in the robin's nest, and three pearls in the grass thimble of the humming bird, speckled eggs in the nest of the hermit thrush in the maple tree, and freckled eggs in the marsh grass where the sandpeep whistles.

It is a wonder now to walk the woods. The leaves are still wrinkled and translucent, and they let the sunlight through. The seven-pointed starflowers float over the forest floor with only the shadow of a thread to hold them above the clustered leaves. From glossy leaves shaped like hearts the Canadian Mayflowers go up like rockets and explode into snowy flowers too small to be believed. The purple bird-on-the-wing flies here fiercely in motionless flight. The bunchberry blooms spread out petals of ivory set on four leaves that are marked like globes with lines of longitude.

The lady's slipper opens her wide-grooved leaves, and up leaps a high stem, and a veined and swollen pink heart floats and beats all by itself in thin air. The speckled thrush hangs to a bough like a flower himself, and his throat swells out big with soft bells going higher and higher into loveliness.

It is May, new leaves and young blossoms, and the year is ready to burst at all seams.

—ROBERT P. TRISTRAM COFFIN

# Mothering Sunday

It is the day of all the year,
Of all the year the one day,
When I shall see my Mother dear
And bring her cheer
A-Mothering Sunday.

So I'll put on my Sunday coat,
And in my hat a feather,
And get the lines I writ by rote,
With many a note,
That I've a-strung together.

And now to fetch my wheaten cake,
To fetch it from the baker,
He promised me, for Mother's sake,
The best he'd bake
For me to fetch and take her.

Well have I known, as I went by,
One hollow lane, that none day
I'd fail to find—for all they're shy—
Where violets lie,
As I went home on Sunday.

My sister Jane is waiting-maid
Along with Squire's lady;
And year by year her part she's played
And home she's stayed,
To get the dinner ready.

For Mother'll come to Church, you'll see—
Of all the year it's the day—
'The one,' she'll say, 'that's made for me.'
And so it be:
It's every Mother's free day.

The boys will all come home from town,
Not one will miss that one day;
And every maid will hustle down
To show her gown,
A-Mothering on Sunday.

It is the day of all the year,
Of all the year the one day;
And here come I, my Mother dear,
To bring you cheer,
A-Mothering on Sunday.

—GERMAN CAROL (FOURTEENTH CENTURY)

# The Day Things Happened

The last Saturday in May began just like an ordinary day. In fact it looked as if it might be a little duller than most; the sun didn't come out till after breakfast. But as the day went on it turned out to be a very important one. At least for Mab.

The first important thing happened when Mab found the handsome little knife with the beautiful blue stone in the handle—the knife her mother had lost in this very same meadow when she was a little girl. Breathless with excitement, Mab raced through the meadow, hurdled over the fence, and dropped down beside her aunt.

"Look, look! Oh, Aunt Belinda, I've found it after all these years!"

In the kitchen they cleaned the knife. It was black and corroded, but there on the handle, unmistakable, was the letter M.

The second important thing happened when Mab took Cato, Aunt Belinda's parrot, out for a walk in the garden. Mab lifted her arm straight from the shoulder, and he walked pigeon-toed down the length of it and balanced on her wrist.

"Mab!" called Aunt Belinda from the house. "Time to set the table, dear, Mab!"

"Mab," said Cato experimentally.

"Why, you know my name!" cried Mab almost dropping him in her excitement. "Cato, darling! Say it again, please say it. Mab. Just like before. Mab."

And he did say it again obligingly: twice in the garden, and then half a dozen times in the kitchen for Aunt Belinda. And after that he shrieked it for three quarters of an hour in his cage.

Later, unexpectedly that afternoon Mab and Candy met Ben Pardee driving along the moor road, and business being slow, he decided to take them for a ride in his taxi. "Entirely free of charge," said Ben grandly, opening the door for them.

The rolling moors were blue as far as the eye could see. Blue with a thick carpet of crowfoot violets! It was beautiful. They all got out. For half an hour they wandered over blue hills and down into blue hollows. The children's hands were full of violets, and Ben had tucked two or three into his cap behind his ear. Once, flanking a low rise they came upon an army of pink moccasin flowers, hundreds of them, tall and proud. So they picked some of those, too.

When Mab reached home with her flowers, Aunt Belinda told her that Miss Fish had telephoned. "She said to tell you that her plant has a big bud on it, and it's going to flower tonight. We must go and see it about nine o'clock."

And that was the last important thing. A little after nine they went up the dark leafy streets, calling for Candy on their way. When they came to the house on Upper Main Street and clonked the knocker, Toto and Mimi could be heard yapping themselves hoarse as usual. But Mab had never been here at night before, and when Mrs. Ellison opened the door for them, she thought that everything looked different; the furniture, the staircase, even Mrs. Ellison and the dogs. Miss Fish's room was different, too. It was lit by a single lamp, and beyond the uncurtained windows the harbor lights glittered on the dark.

"It's almost time for it to open," said Miss Fish in an excited voice. "Look, here it is."

The ugly plant in its pot by the window looked like an untidy bundle of sticks; but there, sure enough, on one of its awkward arms perched a big bud closed in a rosy sheath. Even as they watched, it began to swell.

"In about an hour I should think," said Miss Fish. "I think it's going to be the finest I ever had."

Mab and Candy sat side by side on the edge of the bed, stiff with good manner. Candy kept swallowing one yawn after another till her eyes watered. Aunt Belinda and Miss Fish sat in the chairs (Aunt Belinda knitting) and talked in a foreign, grownup way. By and by Miss Fish produced refreshments—cocoa and little cakes. Candy stopped yawning.

At about ten o'clock Miss Fish looked at her watch and then at the bud, like a doctor taking the pulse of a patient. "It's just about ready," she said. "Mab, will you run down and tell Mrs. Ellison? She wants to see it, too."

Mab flew.

"You're just in time," said Miss Fish when Mab came back with the landlady.

"My, I wouldn't miss this for anything," whispered Mrs. Ellison. It was funny the way they were speaking in low voices, as if they were afraid of disturbing the flower. After that there was hardly any sound in the room except Mrs. Ellison's breathing, which was the breathing of a fat person who has just climbed two flights of stairs. Mab could feel it warmly fanning the back of her neck. They all stood, without a word, staring at the bud as though they expected it to speak to them.

Now slowly, slowly, before their very eyes the flower began to unfold. First one petal, then the next trembled open, like a hand unclosing finger by finger; until at last, frail and exquisite it bloomed in all its perfection. It's like a promise, or a miracle, Mab thought; it's like the Star of Bethlehem.

Candy broke the spell of silence with a gusty sigh of rapture. "Jiminy crickets," she whispered in awe. "Who ever saw anything like that! Did you see how it opened right under our noses like some kind of a magic thing?"

Mab nodded. She was looking into the heart of the flower with its silky fringe of stamens set in a circle of many waxy petals. From it came a perfume more delicate and delicious than any she had ever known.

"And smell it, too." exclaimed Candy, this time with a gusty sniff. "Just smell that thing! I wish you could buy a smell like that in a bottle."

Mab didn't answer. I must make a wish, she thought. It's a sign like the first star, or a rainbow, or the moon over your left shoulder. And tomorrow it will be gone forever. So she made a wish; but it was a secret one.

Clear on the night air came the sound of bells.

"Good heavens, eleven o'clock!" cried Aunt Belinda. "Come, children, we must go."

Mab struggled absentmindedly into her coat, still staring at the flower and learning its shape and color by heart, so she would not forget it.

"Gee, Miss Fish," remarked Candy. "You ought to have just

wonderful dreams going to sleep in the same room with that flower."

"But I'm not going to sleep," Miss Fish told her. "I'm going to sit up all night and keep it company."

"That's exactly what I'd do, too," agreed Mab approvingly.

"Well, next year there'll be another one," said Miss Fish. "And you must come and see it."

"Not for a whole year!" said Candy. It was practically a lifetime.

Mab and Aunt Belinda left Candy at her house and walked on. Mab tucked her arm into her aunt's; their footsteps made a lonely sound on the stret. A fog crept in from the sea, and all the street-lamps had gold halos like tall, thin saints. From far away came the banshee voice of the foghorn. The air was damp and warm and smelled of leaves. Mab thought about the flower and her mother's knife and Cato saying her name. She thought how school would soon be over. Pretty soon it would be warm enough for swimming, too. Slowly, slowly, the summer was unfolding; emerging from the harsh gray stalk of winter. It was opening outward day by day, till at last it would be whole and perfect as the flower on Miss Fish's plant.

—FROM *The Day Things Happened*
BY ELIZABETH ENRIGHT

# Memorial Day

Memorial Day honors those who have fallen in battle fighting for our country. On May 30, many gather to pay tribute, to decorate the graves, and to offer prayers for peace and goodwill throughout the world.

During and after the Civil War women began decorating with flowers the graves in the military cemeteries. The practice spread until today in most states May 30 is a legal holiday. On this day the flag is flown at half-staff until noon, from then until sunset at full staff.

The pledge of allegiance to the flag was first written for school children observing Memorial Day in Wisconsin.

Memorial Day is a sober, thought-provoking day. Much has been written about the debt we owe to those who gave their lives in wars.

—MILDRED CORELL LUCKHARDT

# The Debt

When we have given to earth's stricken lands
The service of our minds and hearts and hands,
When we have made the blackened orchards bright,
And brought the homeless ones to warmth and light,
When we have made these desolate forget,
We shall have paid a little of our debt.

—THEODOSIA GARRISON

# Concord Hymn

Spirit, that made those heroes dare
To die, and leave their children free,
Bid Time and Nature gently spare
The shaft we raise to them and thee.

—LINES FROM *"Concord Hymn"*
BY RALPH WALDO EMERSON

# What Is So Rare as a Day in June?

And what is so rare as a day in June?
   Then, if ever, come perfect days;
Then Heaven tries earth if it be in tune,
   And over it softly her warm ear lays.
Whether we look, or whether we listen,
   We hear life murmur, or see it glisten;
Every clod feels a stir of might,
   An instinct within it that reaches and towers,
And, groping blindly above it for light,
   Climbs to a soul in grass and flowers;
The flush of life may well be seen
   Thrilling back over hills and valleys;
The cowslip startles in meadows green,
   The buttercup catches the sun in its chalice,
And there's never a leaf nor a blade too mean
   To be some happy creature's palace;
The little bird sits at his door in the sun,
   Atilt like a blossom among the leaves,
And lets his illumined being o'errun
   With the deluge of summer it receives;
His mate feels the eggs beneath her wings,
And the heart in her dumb breast flutters and sings;
He sings to the wide world, and she to her nest,—
In the nice ear of Nature which song is the best?

            —FROM *The Vision of Sir Launfal*
               BY JAMES RUSSELL LOWELL

# Daisies

Over the shoulders and slopes of the dune
   I saw the white daisies go down to the sea,
A host in the sunshine, an army in June,
   The people God sends us to set our heart free.

The bobolinks rallied them up from the dell,
   The orioles whistled them out of the wood;
And all of their singing was "Earth, it is well!"
   And all of their dancing was, "Life, thou art good!"
          —FROM *Songs from Vagabondia*
             BY BLISS CARMAN


# Daisies

Where innocent bright-eyed daisies are
   With blades of grass between,
Each daisy stands up like a star
   Out of a sky of green.
          —CHRISTINA ROSSETTI

# Acadia

And when mild Spring, with all her magic powers,
Spreads o'er the land her simple robe of flowers,
And clad in green thy teeming vales appear,
Oh! then, Acadia, thou art doubly dear . . .
For, though Acadia's sons may stray at times
To lands more fruitful, and to milder climes,
The exile pines to tread his native land;
Her fertile valleys and her lovely forms,
Crowd on the mind with dreams of mighty power,
And cheer his heart in many a lonely hour.

—LINES FROM *"Acadia"* BY

JOSEPH HOWE

# Flag Day
## *June 14*

On June 14, 1777, in the midst of the Revolutionary War, the Continental Congress resolved that "The flag of the United States will be thirteen stripes alternate red and white, that the union be thirteen stars white in a blue field representing a new constellation." Thus the flag of the United States of America was born.

Tradition holds that Mrs. Betsy Griscom Ross, a Philadelphia widow noted for making flags, was asked by General George Washington and George Ross and Robert Morris, members of the Continental Congress, to make the new flag.

Many changes have occurred. Millions from all over the world have come to be citizens and "pledge allegiance to the flag of the United States of America." Probably no one who saw those thirteen stars for thirteen colonies ever dreamed that some day half a hundred stars would symbolize one of the most powerful of nations.

In 1877 the Congress of the United States asked that all the public fly the American flag on June 14 to honor the hundredth anniversary of the American flag. Through the years the people continued to observe the day until in 1949 Congress made June 14 the official Flag Day.

For important days and for special ceremonies, those who raise their country's flag share a great sense of pride and loyalty, and of responsibility, too. George Rebh, a student, defines those feelings in the story, "The Flag-Raising," which follows.

—MILDRED CORELL LUCKHARDT

# The Flag-Raising

This was the day which had captured the thoughts and dreams of the eleven young Cub Scouts of Den Three. This was their chance to show everyone in that large stadium why Den Three was the best den in all of that big city. The time was soon approaching when all eleven Cub Scouts would march across the diamond of the very large stadium and raise the American Flag to signify the beginning of another baseball season.

As the boys waited in a room under the stands, an air of uneasiness dominated the movements of the smartly dressed eleven. But one Scout was more apprehensive than the others. He was John Taylor, and he was to be the boy to actually raise the flag—he was to be the subject of all those carefully focused eyes.

John's mind was filled with visions of the flag-raising. He imagined himself dropping the flag, and he thought how horrible that would be. So many people were going to watch him! His throat became steadily drier, and he rubbed together his already wet palms. His joints seemed to stiffen, and now his knees began to shake. With the time for the ceremonies drawing near, John looked into the eyes of his ten fellow Scouts and forced a smile.

338

As the boys marched across the bright green field, the buzzing of the crowd grew louder, but John could not hear a thing. He was looking at the tall pole ahead, which now seemed to loom over him as a fierce and overpowering force. He took a fleeting glance at the many different colors which spotted the large stadium. Nearing the pole, John tightened his grasp on the folded flag.

Having connected the small metal eyes of the flag to the hooks on the rope which dangled earthward, John began to raise the flag, on the seemingly sky-piercing pole. The band started to play, but he could only faintly hear it; all his senses were trained on the flag, which was slowly climbing the tall pole. Methodically, John pulled the rope—a pull with one hand, and then a pull with the other. He made sure of each grasp.

His heart was beating violently, and his head gradually tilted backward, watching the colors rise. Suddenly, with his arms now drained of strength, he felt a jerk—the flag had reached the top of the pole! Carefully tying the rope to the side of the pole, John looked at his ten friends and smiled.

One of the boys came over to where John stood and said, "Way to go, Johnny!" And now, as the band's music met John's awakened ears, he gazed at the approving crowd, and then up at the proud flag which rippled in the breeze. And his knees ceased shaking. He stood straight and tall with one more upward look at his country's flag.

—GEORGE REBH, *Spectrum*, HUNTSVILLE HIGH SCHOOL,

HUNTSVILLE, ALABAMA, 1968

# William Tell
## (*A Story for Father's Day*)

His father's steps were long, swift, and evenly spaced. Sometimes Walter had to run to keep up. But he ran eagerly and with pride. He liked being the son of William Tell, who was known throughout the countryside for his skill with the crossbow and arrows. Just now, when their beloved Switzerland was attempting to free itself from the tyranny of Austria, William Tell was known also as a patriot of great bravery and daring. As he thought of it, Walter threw his shoulders back and measured his paces; and then, somehow, his eyes went upward toward the great mountaintops.

"Father," he called, "must we hurry so? Is it true that the trees on the mountaintop will bleed if struck with an axe?"

His father slowed his steps and smiled. "Who says so, boy?"

"The herdsman, Father. He says there's a charm on the trees, and if a man injures one of them, the hand that strikes the blow will grow out from the grave."

"That's a very old legend, Son. If 'tis true I know not, but if there were no trees, the avalanches of snow and ice from the mountaintops would long ago have destroyed the villages hereabout. Would that the trees could protect us also from Austria—"

"Are there countries with no mountains, Father?"

"Yes, if we travel downward from our heights, we reach a wide and level country where our mountain torrents brawl and foam no more; where great rivers glide serenely on. From those plains all the heavens may be seen. Spring is there already, and all the land is like a garden fair."

"Do you like that country better than our mountains?" Walter asked in great surprise.

"Ah, no," laughed William Tell. "There's almost nothing I like better than our mountains. Next to your mother, your brother, and you, I love Switzerland."

Walter thought of his younger brother with a slight feeling of guilt. It must be very disappointing to be so young and not be allowed to go into the village with Father.

"Why are we going to Altdorf, Father?" asked Walter.

"I must see your grandfather. There is to be a meeting of the patriots—"

"Father, isn't Herr Gessler in Altdorf?"

"Yes, he is in the village. How did you know?"

"The herdsman was talking. He said—"

"Learn not to repeat gossip, Walter; it can be very dangerous. Yes, Gessler the shrewd, Gessler the cruel, Gessler, the Austrian king's strutting, swaggering bailiff, is in our village. He has set up a pole in the marketplace. And on the pole he has hung a hat, the emblem of Austrian power. All who pass must do homage to that hat." William Tell's voice was strong and sharp, but it was as if he were talking to himself. At first, he seemed not to hear when Walter spoke.

"Will you bow when you go past the hat?" Walter asked.

"What's that? Of course I won't—but, wait. Your mother was right. I should not have allowed you to come with me today."

"Ha! I afraid?" Walter asked. "The son of William Tell?"

"I should have listened to your mother," his father said, though he smiled at Walter. "Now, hear me, boy. We are approaching the village. As we walk through the marketplace, look neither to the right nor to the left. And stay close behind me."

"Look, Father," Walter cried as they came into the marketplace. "There's the pole with the hat on it!"

"We're going to your grandfather's," his father murmured. "Stay close behind me."

"But there's grandfather, standing just beside the fountain."

"So it is," said William Tell, "and, note you, we have passed the pole with the hat on it."

But a soldier had stepped from beside the pole. "Stop," he said. "I command you to stop in the name of the king."

"Why do you stop me?" asked Tell.

"You have broken the mandate. You have not done obeisance to the hat. Come with me." The soldier pinned Tell's arms behind him.

"Let me go," Tell said as he struggled. "Let me go now."

"Not so fast," said the soldier. "You are going to but one place. Prison."

"Prison?" cried Walter. "Grandfather, come quickly. They are taking my father to prison." At the sound of Walter's voice his father attempted to turn his head to speak to him.

"Go to your grandfather, Walter. He will see that you get home safely. Tell your mother—" but the soldier jerked him away.

Suddenly, the marketplace was swarming with villagers and soldiers of the king. "What goes on here?" asked a friend of William Tell. "What are they doing to William?" asked Walter's grandfather as he rushed toward Walter and William Tell. "He is a traitor," said one of the soldiers, "an enemy of the king."

"He is William Tell," said the villagers proudly. "He can run faster than the wind and shoot a bow and arrow like no other man."

"Oh, he can, can he?" said a jeering, sneering voice. It was Gessler, the king's bailiff. "If that is true, he will have an opportunity to prove it."

"He's very good," said Walter. "He will shoot an apple off a tree for you—a tree a hundred yards away."

"How very nice," said the bailiff, and then, to Walter, "Who are you?"

"I'm Walter, son of William Tell."

"Come, William Tell," said Gessler, "since you can bring down an apple from a tree, prove your skill before me. Take your bow, and shoot an apple from this stripling's head."

The soldiers who had been holding William Tell pushed him forward. "Please, my lord," Tell spoke in a hoarse whisper, "can you ask this? That I shoot an apple from the head of my beloved son? He is but a boy. Rather let me die, my lord. You cannot ask—"

Gessler smiled. "I not only ask it, I command it. You must shoot or with you dies the boy." Turning to the soldiers, Gessler spoke quickly, "Bind the boy to yonder tree."

"You need not bind me," shouted Walter. "I can stand. I am not afraid."

"Walter," his father cried. "Walter, my son, come back."

But Walter had already taken his place beneath the tree.

"Look," some of the people murmured, "look at William Tell. His hands are trembling. What monstrous things these Austrians do."

"Take your distance, Tell," ordered Gessler. "Mind you, be sure you are eighty paces from the tree. See? I ask not a hundred. Only eighty. But, wait, as one more evidence of the king's mercy, we will bind the boy's eyes."

"No, no!" shouted Walter. "Do not bind my eyes. Do you think I fear an arrow from my father's bow? Quickly, Father, shoot!"

The apple that had been placed on his head by one of the king's soldiers moved not at all as the boy spoke.

William Tell turned once more to Gessler. "Release me, I beg of you. Release me from this shot."

Gessler smiled. "Now, Master Bowman, would you have me think you cannot perform this feat? You? The hope of all Switzerland?"

Even as Gessler spoke, Tell's arrow whistled through the air. The crowd made not a sound. Moments later the silence was broken by Walter's exultant cry:: "Here are the pieces of the apple, Father. I knew you would not hit me."

"By heaven," said Gessler, "the apple's cleft right through the core. It was a master shot, I must allow."

A villager answer him, "True, the shot was good. But woe to him who drove the man to tempt his God by such a feat."

"I would have a word with you, Tell," said Gessler.

"What can you possibly have to say to me?" asked William Tell, hugging his son to his side.

"I saw," said Gessler, "a second arrow in your belt. Do not deny it. I saw it well. What was its purpose? For an honest answer, I will give you your life."

"My life?" asked Tell. "For an honest answer? Well, my lord, if my hand had slipped and I had struck my child, that second arrow was for you."

In the years which followed, Switzerland freed itself of its enemies. It forgot the old wounds and the hatreds, and the country of the mountaintops has remained a peaceful, pleasant place. Throughout the world people have told with love and admiration the story of William Tell and his son.

—ADAPTED FROM THE TRANSLATION

OF SIR THEODORE MARTIN OF THE WORK

BY JOHANN C. F. VON SCHILLER

# Out in the Fields with God

The little cares that fretted me,
  I lost them yesterday
Among the fields above the sea,
  Among the winds at play;
Among the lowing herds,
  The rustling of the trees,
Among the singing birds,
  The humming of the bees.

The fears of what may come to pass
  I cast them all away,
Among the clover-scented grass,
  Among the new-mown hay;
Among the hushing of the corn,
  Where drowsy poppies nod,
Where ill thoughts die and good are born,
  Out in the fields with God.

—AUTHOR UNKNOWN

# A Prayer in Spring

Oh, give us pleasure in the flowers today;
And give us not to think so far away
As the uncertain harvest; keep us here
All simply in the springing of the year.

Oh, give us pleasure in the orchard white,
Like nothing else by day, like ghosts by night;
And make us happy in the happy bees,
The swarm dilating round the perfect trees.

And make us happy in the darting bird
That suddenly above the bees is heard,
The meteor that thrusts in with needle bill,
And off a blossom in mid air stands still.

For this is love and nothing else is love,
The which it is reserved for God above
To sanctify to what far ends He will,
But which it only needs that we fulfil.

—ROBERT FROST

# INDEX